PRACTICE BOOK

VOYAGES
IN ENGLISH
GRAMMAR AND WRITING

3

LOYOLAPRESS.

Cover Design: Judine O'Shea
Cover Art: Pablo Bernasconi
Interior Design: Think Book Works
Editor: Pamela Jennett

ISBN-13: 978-0-8294-2828-5
ISBN-10: 0-8294-2828-3

© 2011 Loyola Press
All rights reserved. No part of this book may be reproduced, stored in a retrieval system, or
transmitted in any form or by any means, electronic, mechanical, photocopying, recording,
or otherwise, without the prior permission of the publisher.

LOYOLA PRESS.
3441 N. Ashland Avenue
Chicago, Illinois 60657
(800) 621-1008
www.loyolapress.com

19 20 21 22 23 24 25 26 27 LSC 15 14 13 12 11 10 9 8 7

Contents

GRAMMAR

WRITING

SECTION 1 Daily Maintenance

1.1 Mary walks the dogs.

1. What is the proper noun?   _____

2. What is the plural noun?   _____

3. Which word is a verb?   _____

4. Diagram the sentence here.

1.2 We saw a tall giraffe.

1. Is *We* a noun or a pronoun?   _____

2. What is the verb?   _____

3. Which word describes *giraffe*?   _____

4. Diagram the sentence here.

1.3 The boys build a fort.

1. What is the singular noun?   _____

2. What is the plural noun?   _____

3. What is the verb?   _____

4. Diagram the sentence here.

© Loyola Press. Voyages in English   Grade 3

1.4 **I baked a delicious pie.**

1. Is *I* a noun or a pronoun?   _____

2. What is the verb?   _____

3. What does *delicious* describe?   _____

4. Diagram the sentence here.

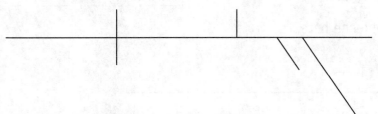

1.5 **He made two strikes.**

1. Is this sentence a statement or a question?   _____

2. Which word is the verb?   _____

3. Which word tells how many?   _____

4. Diagram the sentence here.

1.6 **The red dress is beautiful.**

1. Is this sentence a statement or a command?   _____

2. Which word is a verb?   _____

3. Is the verb an action verb or a linking verb?   _____

4. Diagram the sentence here.

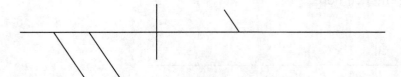

© Loyola Press. Voyages in English   Grade 3

1.7 **The black plums are juicy.**

1. Is this sentence a statement or a question? _____

2. What is the verb? _____

3. Which words are adjectives? _____

4. Diagram the sentence here.

1.8 **The children petted the goat.**

1. What is the complete subject? _____

2. Which word is a verb? _____

3. Is *children* a singular noun or a plural noun? _____

4. Diagram the sentence here.

1.9 **Sam found a small feather.**

1. What is the simple subject? _____

2. What is the simple predicate? _____

3. Which word is an adjective? _____

4. Diagram the sentence here.

© Loyola Press. Voyages in English   Grade 3

1.10 **Cara rides a new bicycle.**

1. Is *Cara* the subject or the verb? _____

2. Which word is a common noun? _____

3. What does *new* describe? _____

4. Diagram the sentence here.

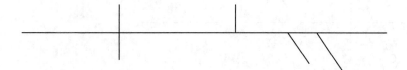

1.11 **They picked red apples.**

1. What is the complete subject? _____

2. What is the complete predicate? _____

3. Is *They* a noun or a pronoun? _____

4. Diagram the sentence here.

© Loyola Press. Voyages in English   Grade 3

1.1 Sentences

A **sentence** is a group of words that expresses a complete thought. Every sentence has a subject that names a person, a place, or a thing. Every sentence has a predicate that tells what the subject is or does.

Add a period after each word group that is a complete sentence. Cross out each word group that is not a sentence.

1. Claire feeds my fish
2. Beautiful pine trees on the mountains
3. Oscar draws in art class
4. We sat in the shade
5. The green grass
6. Atlanta is a large city
7. Liu's cat hid under the bed
8. A bird is sitting on the sign
9. Is next door to my house
10. Ran across the field

Add a subject or a predicate to each word group to make a sentence.

11. the gray horse

_____

12. a fire engine

_____

13. played in the sand

_____

Write two sentences. Write one about yourself and one about a friend.

14. _____

15. _____

© Loyola Press. Voyages in English   Grade 3

For additional help, review pages 2–3 in your textbook or visit www.voyagesinenglish.com.

1.2 Statements and Questions

A telling sentence is called a **statement.** It ends with a period.
An asking sentence is called a **question.** It ends with a question mark.
Both kinds of sentences begin with a capital letter.

Add a period at the end of each statement. Add a question mark at the end of each question.

1. I went to the zoo with my friend
2. Did you hear the lion roar
3. I ate popcorn and peanuts
4. The sun was shining
5. Where were the lizards and snakes
6. How many animals did you see
7. Antonio saw a giraffe for the first time
8. What did you like best about the zoo
9. I liked the penguins best
10. We rode the bus home

Write the letter of the words that complete each sentence.

11. I ride _____   a. opens the door for each student.
12. How many _____   b. the bus to school.
13. Mr. Wilson _____   c. rumbles down the road.
14. The bus driver _____   d. children ride the bus?
15. The bus _____   e. is the bus driver.
16. Who sits _____   f. next to you on the bus?

Write a statement and a question.

17. Statement: _____
18. Question: _____

© Loyola Press. Voyages in English   Grade 3

For additional help, review pages 4–5 in your textbook
or visit www.voyagesinenglish.com.

1.3 Question Words

A question often starts with a **question word.** *Who, what, when, where, why,* and *how* are some question words.

Circle the question word that correctly completes each sentence.

1. (Who   Where) are the markers I bought?

2. (What   When) will the baseball game begin?

3. (Where   What) did you bring for the picnic?

4. (How   Who) did the plumber fix the sink?

5. (When   Who) is the man talking to our teacher?

6. (Why   When) do plants need sunlight?

7. (Where   What) should I put my backpack?

Write *who, what, when, where, why,* or *how* to complete each sentence.

8. _____ is the Statue of Liberty located?

9. _____ does the concert begin?

10. _____ is coming to the party?

11. _____ did you get for your birthday?

12. _____ were you late for school today?

13. _____ do you get to school each day?

Write a question that you might ask each person. Use the question word in parentheses.

14. your teacher (When)

_____

15. the president of the United States (What)

_____

16. a veterinarian (How)

_____

For additional help, review pages 6–7 in your textbook or visit www.voyagesinenglish.com.

Section 1 • 7

© Loyola Press. Voyages in English   Grade 3

1.4 Commands

A **command** is a sentence that tells a person what to do. The subject of a command is *you*. The subject is not stated in most commands. A command ends with a period.

Circle *C* (command), *S* (statement), or *Q* (question) to identify each sentence.

1. Listen to your teacher.   C   S   Q

2. Tamika, did you walk the dog?   C   S   Q

3. Take out the garbage, Pat.   C   S   Q

4. I heard thunder yesterday.   C   S   Q

5. Are you ready to go to the library?   C   S   Q

6. Please push in the chair.   C   S   Q

7. Kwan painted a beautiful picture.   C   S   Q

8. Did you help clean the kitchen?   C   S   Q

Change each sentence into a command.

9. You need to fill the bucket with water.

_____

10. You have to return your library books today.

_____

11. You should put those dishes in the sink.

_____

12. You have to fold the paper into fourths.

_____

Write two commands that you might hear at school or at home.

13. _____

14. _____

© Loyola Press. Voyages in English   Grade 3

For additional help, review pages 8–9 in your textbook or visit www.voyagesinenglish.com.

1.5 Exclamations

An **exclamation** is a sentence that expresses strong or sudden emotion. An exclamation ends with an exclamation point.

Add an exclamation point to each sentence that is an exclamation.

1. I wanted to see the two giraffes

2. How tall they are

3. Do you see the pandas

4. What a cute cub that is

5. The lions are sleeping in the shade

6. I like the tigers best

7. Yikes, that python is huge

8. Wow, look at the crocodile's sharp teeth

Circle the emotion expressed in each exclamation.

9. That was the best birthday ever!   worry   happiness

10. How amazing the Grand Canyon is!   wonder   fear

11. Oh no, I broke my favorite cup!   worry   respect

12. Wow, I never knew these plants lived in the desert!   fear   surprise

13. What a spooky, old house this is!   fear   happiness

Imagine that it is a stormy day. Finish each exclamation with words that show strong emotion. Add an exclamation point.

14. A big storm _____

15. How strong the wind _____

16. Oh no, the wind _____

17. Hurry, it's _____

18. What a loud _____

19. The lightning really _____

© Loyola Press. Voyages in English   Grade 3

For additional help, review pages 10–11 in your textbook or visit www.voyagesinenglish.com.

1.6 Kinds of Sentences

A **statement** tells something. A **question** asks something. A **command** gives a direction. An **exclamation** expresses a strong or a sudden feeling. Each kind of sentence ends with the correct punctuation.

Write *statement*, *question*, *command*, or *exclamation* to identify each sentence.

1. My family is visiting a pet store. _____

2. How cute these bunnies are! _____

3. What kind of pet do you want? _____

4. I want a brown and white guinea pig. _____

5. Look at the guinea pigs in this cage. _____

6. We will buy the dark brown one. _____

7. What should we name her? _____

8. We will name her Chocolate. _____

Add the correct end punctuation to each sentence.

9. We are planting a garden

10. Where should I plant the roses

11. Bring me that shovel

12. What vegetable is this

13. I will plant the tulips here

14. How beautiful our garden is

15. These purple flowers are my favorites

Rewrite the sentence as a command and as a question.

16. Your red jacket is in the closet.

_____

_____

© Loyola Press. Voyages in English Grade 3

For additional help, review pages 12–13 in your textbook or visit www.voyagesinenglish.com.

1.6 Kinds of Sentences

A sentence can be a **statement**, a **question**, a **command**, or an **exclamation.** Each kind of sentence ends with the correct punctuation.

Write *statement*, *question*, *command*, or *exclamation* to tell about each sentence. Then add the correct end punctuation to each sentence.

1. Please turn to page 75   _____

2. Who is the author of the story   _____

3. The author is Sandra Cisneros   _____

4. Who is the main character   _____

5. This story is about a young girl   _____

6. Discuss the ending with a partner   _____

7. What an exciting story that was   _____

8. Gosh, I was not expecting that ending   _____

Rewrite each sentence with the correct end punctuation.

9. Where did you leave your backpack.

_____

10. Yikes, I missed the bus.

_____

11. Review your notes before the test?

_____

Use the directions to write each sentence.

12. Write a command spoken by a librarian.

_____

13. Write an exclamation spoken by a sports fan.

_____

© Loyola Press. Voyages in English   Grade 3

For additional help, review pages 12–13 in your textbook or visit www.voyagesinenglish.com.

Section 1 • 11

1.7 Subjects

The **subject** is who or what the sentence is about. The **simple subject** names the person, place, or thing that is talked about. The **complete subject** is the simple subject and any words that describe it.

Underline the complete subject in each sentence.

1. Javier ran around the track.

2. My papers fell into the puddle.

3. The children went to the museum.

4. Greg found a dollar on the sidewalk.

5. The ball flew through the air.

6. Our class reads the newspaper every day.

7. Katie bought a new blouse.

8. Many gray squirrels ran through the yard.

9. The heavy book is a dictionary.

Write whether the underlined text is the *complete subject* or the *simple subject* of the sentence.

10. My <u>sister</u> is in a band. _____

11. <u>Nikki</u> plays the guitar and sings. _____

12. The <u>band</u> practices in our garage. _____

13. <u>Our neighbors</u> do not mind the noise. _____

14. <u>Many people</u> enjoy the band's music. _____

Write a complete subject that finishes each sentence.

15. _____ builds a sand castle.

16. _____ swim in the ocean.

17. _____ finds a small crab on the beach.

18. _____ sail across the water.

© Loyola Press. Voyages in English   Grade 3

For additional help, review pages 14–15 in your textbook or visit www.voyagesinenglish.com.

1.8 Predicates

The **predicate** tells what the subject is or does. The **simple predicate** is a verb that expresses an action or a state of being. The **complete predicate** is the simple predicate and any words that describe it.

Underline the complete predicate in each sentence.

1. Ryan has piano lessons after school.

2. The bird escaped from its cage.

3. Rashad and Troy raced to the top of the hill.

4. Dad cooked dinner last night.

5. The art teacher used pinecones for the bird feeders.

6. My cousin is a good reader.

7. I yanked on the rope.

8. Snowflakes land on my nose.

9. My grandmother knits soft scarves.

Underline the complete predicate in each sentence. Then write the simple predicate.

10. Sarah looks through her closet.   _____

11. She finds her old toys and books.   _____

12. Sarah's family holds a yard sale.   _____

13. Many people come to the sale.   _____

14. Sarah's neighbors buy some stuffed animals.   _____

15. Sarah sells all her toys and books.   _____

Write a complete predicate that finishes each sentence.

16. My family _____.

17. Our dog _____.

18. This store _____.

19. A noisy bird _____.

© Loyola Press. Voyages in English   Grade 3

For additional help, review pages 16–17 in your textbook or visit www.voyagesinenglish.com.

1.9 Combining Subjects and Predicates

If two sentences have the same subject or same predicate, they can often be combined. Two subjects or two predicates can be joined by the words *and, but,* or *or* to make a **compound subject** or **compound predicate.**

Combine the predicates to write one sentence.

1. The children whispered. The children giggled.

   _____

2. Mrs. Andrews sat down. Mrs. Andrews opened her book.

   _____

3. The dentist cleaned my teeth. The dentist filled a cavity.

   _____

4. My father trimmed the tree. My father watered the lawn.

   _____

Combine the subjects to write one sentence.

5. Mom washed the dishes. I washed the dishes.

   _____

6. Luke likes football. Tom likes football.

   _____

7. My brother walked the dogs. My sister walked the dogs.

   _____

8. My aunt lives in Florida. My cousins live in Florida.

   _____

Write two sentences, one with two subjects and one with two predicates.

9. _____

10. _____

© Loyola Press. Voyages in English **Grade 3**

For additional help, review pages 18–19 in your textbook or visit www.voyagesinenglish.com.

1.10 Combining Sentences

A **compound sentence** contains two short sentences joined by *and, but,* or *or*. To combine two short sentences into one longer sentence, add a comma followed by *and, but,* or *or*.

Combine each pair of sentences into a compound sentence.

1. Jay made the salad. Megan set the table.

_____

2. My older brother can drive. I have to take the bus.

_____

3. My friends brought the food. I brought the games.

_____

4. The movie started on time. We were late.

_____

5. I will make tacos. I will bring chicken.

_____

Write the letter of a sentence in Column B that matches each sentence in Column A to make a compound sentence.

COLUMN A

6. My family has many games, and _____
7. I want to play checkers, but _____
8. Mom sets up the board, but _____
9. Jeff tries hard to win, but _____

COLUMN B

a. Dad always beats him at chess.
b. Helen wants to play dominoes.
c. we have family game night on Friday.
d. she can't find all the game pieces.

Write a short sentence to complete each compound sentence.

10. Lily might watch a movie, or _____.

11. I like scary stories, but _____.

12. Dark clouds filled the sky, and _____.

For additional help, review pages 20–21 in your textbook or visit www.voyagesinenglish.com.

© Loyola Press. Voyages in English Grade 3

Section 1 • 15

1.11 Run-on Sentences

A **run-on sentence** has two or more sentences that are put together without the proper connector. Most run-ons can be fixed by adding *and*, *but*, or *or* after the comma to make a compound sentence.

Write whether each sentence is a *run-on* or *correct*.

1. I brought the gift, and Mom wrapped it.   _____

2. My best friend moved, but we still call each other.   _____

3. Jaime writes music, she plays piano.   _____

4. The team ran on the field, the crowd cheered.   _____

5. Bob found a wallet, he told his teacher.   _____

6. Some students made posters, and others made signs.   _____

7. The windows rattled, a jet flew overhead.   _____

Rewrite each run-on sentence. Add *and, but,* or *or* to make a compound sentence.

8. I have a bicycle, it is blue and red.

   _____

9. We went to the zoo, we saw a baby elephant.

   _____

10. The children can paint pictures, they can read books.

    _____

11. I want to play soccer, I do not have a ball.

    _____

Write two compound sentences. Use correct punctuation and a connector.

12. _____

13. _____

© Loyola Press. Voyages in English   Grade 3

For additional help, review pages 22–23 in your textbook or visit www.voyagesinenglish.com.

SECTION 2   Daily Maintenance

2.1   **The students read books.**

1. What part of speech is *students*?   _____

2. Which word is a verb?   _____

3. Is the sentence a statement or a question?   _____

4. Diagram the sentence here.

2.2   **Jacob buys a red truck.**

1. Is *Jacob* a common noun or a proper noun?   _____

2. Which other word is a noun?   _____

3. What part of speech is *red*?   _____

4. Diagram the sentence here.

2.3   **She plays the piano.**

1. What part of speech is *She*?   _____

2. Is the verb present tense or past tense?   _____

3. Is the sentence a command or a statement?   _____

4. Diagram the sentence here.

© Loyola Press. Voyages in English   Grade 3

2.4 **The spider spins a web.**

1. What is the complete subject?   _____

2. What part of speech is *spins*?   _____

3. Is *web* a singular noun or a plural noun?   _____

4. Diagram the sentence here.

2.5 **Kyle has an older brother.**

1. Which word is a verb?   _____

2. Which word is a comparative adjective?   _____

3. What is the subject?   _____

4. Diagram the sentence here.

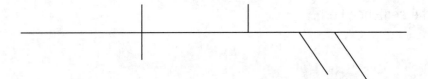

2.6 **The children drink cold lemonade.**

1. Which word is an adjective?   _____

2. What is the simple subject?   _____

3. What part of speech is *drink*?   _____

4. Diagram the sentence here.

© Loyola Press. Voyages in English **Grade 3**

2.7 **Jenna folded the clean towels.**

1. Which word is a plural noun? _____

2. Is the verb present tense or past tense? _____

3. What is the simple predicate? _____

4. Diagram the sentence here.

2.8 **They need two movie tickets.**

1. What part of speech is *two*? _____

2. Is the pronoun singular or plural? _____

3. What is the complete predicate? _____

4. Diagram the sentence here.

2.9 **I wrapped the birthday gift.**

1. What part of speech is the subject? _____

2. Is the verb regular or irregular? _____

3. Which word is an adjective? _____

4. Diagram the sentence here.

© Loyola Press. Voyages in English   Grade 3

2.10 **The birds build a nest.**

1. Which word is a singular noun?   _____

2. What is the complete subject?   _____

3. Is the verb present tense or past tense? _____

4. Diagram the sentence here.

2.11 **He holds the smallest kitten.**

1. Is the pronoun singular or plural?   _____

2. Which word is an adjective?   _____

3. What is the simple predicate?   _____

4. Diagram the sentence here.

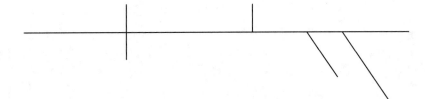

© Loyola Press. Voyages in English   Grade 3

2.1 Nouns

A **noun** is a word that names a person, a place, or a thing.

Write whether each noun is a *person*, a *place*, or a *thing*.

1. spoon _____
2. pilot _____
3. cashier _____
4. Alaska _____
5. Maria _____
6. hospital _____

7. auditorium _____
8. dictionary _____
9. microwave _____
10. bathroom _____
11. photograph _____
12. uncle _____

Underline the nouns in each sentence. The number of nouns in each sentence is in parentheses.

13. Pineapples grow on that island. (2)

14. The grass in the park turned brown. (2)

15. Did the boys visit Mexico? (2)

16. I bought peanuts and popcorn at the game. (3)

17. Mrs. Ramirez works at the airport. (2)

18. The van has seats for eight passengers. (3)

19. Their family lives on a farm in Iowa. (3)

20. Hailey put the pot in the kitchen. (3)

21. My mother buys fresh bread at the bakery. (3)

22. Mario does his homework at the desk in the corner. (4)

Write a sentence using a noun that names each of the following.

23. a person _____

24. a place _____

25. a thing _____

© Loyola Press. Voyages in English   Grade 3

For additional help, review pages 28–29 in your textbook or visit www.voyagesinenglish.com.

2.2 Common and Proper Nouns

A **proper noun** names a particular person, place, or thing. A **common noun** names any one member of a group of people, places, or things.

Write whether each noun is a *common noun* or a *proper noun*.

1. New Mexico _____
2. mountain _____
3. Cinderella _____
4. France _____
5. month _____
6. Monday _____

7. principal _____
8. singer _____
9. Nile River _____
10. J. K. Rowling _____
11. athlete _____
12. Mr. McCoy _____

Underline the common nouns and circle the proper nouns in the sentences.

13. My favorite actor is John Wayne.
14. Who is the current president of the United States?
15. My younger sister enjoys reading Dr. Seuss.
16. Mr. Evans is the new coach of our team.
17. Her cousins live near Niagara Falls.

Write two proper nouns for each common noun.

18. city _____ _____
19. author _____ _____
20. continent _____ _____
21. book character _____ _____
22. president _____ _____
23. band _____ _____
24. park _____ _____
25. movie _____ _____

© Loyola Press. Voyages in English Grade 3

For additional help, review pages 30–31 in your textbook or visit www.voyagesinenglish.com.

2.3 Singular and Plural Nouns

A **singular noun** names one person, place, or thing. A **plural noun** names more than one person, place, or thing.

Write whether each underlined noun is a *singular noun* or a *plural noun*.

1. Jake and his family clean the <u>yard</u>. _____

2. Jake's dad trims the <u>trees</u>. _____

3. The <u>branches</u> fall to the ground. _____

4. Jake picks up the <u>pinecones</u>. _____

5. He puts them in a large garbage <u>bag</u>. _____

6. Jake's mom pulls <u>weeds</u> from the ground. _____

Write the plural for each singular noun.

7. school _____   12. fox _____

8. ladder _____   13. ash _____

9. dress _____   14. tent _____

10. glass _____   15. switch _____

11. lunch _____   16. pumpkin _____

Complete each sentence with the singular or plural form of the noun in parentheses.

17. We need five _____ for the pie. (peach)

18. Many _____ stop at this station every day. (train)

19. I washed the _____ after dinner. (dish)

20. Ashley put one more _____ on the bed. (blanket)

21. We saw playful _____ at the zoo. (penguin)

22. I cannot find my old _____. (backpack)

23. We put our old toys in _____ and stored them in the garage. (box)

24. There are two new _____ in our class. (student)

For additional help, review pages 32–33 in your textbook or visit www.voyagesinenglish.com.

Section 2 • 23

© Loyola Press. Voyages in English   Grade 3

2.4 More Plural Nouns

> To form the plural of a noun ending in a consonant followed by *y*, change the *y* to *i* and add *-es*. For nouns ending in a vowel and *y*, just add *-s*.

Underline the singular nouns and circle the plural nouns in each sentence.

1. The train passes by several towns.

2. The cats often sleep under the bushes.

3. Two donkeys pull each cart to the marketplace.

4. Tall sunflowers grow in our garden.

5. I put strawberries on my pancakes.

6. Both girls got new dresses.

7. The bunnies munch on carrots.

8. How many years are in a century?

9. Our families camp at the lake every summer.

10. The boys walked their puppies to the park.

Write the plural for each singular noun.

11. pony _____   16. body _____

12. toy _____   17. party _____

13. ray _____   18. fly _____

14. story _____   19. gallery _____

15. tray _____   20. charity _____

Rewrite each sentence. Write the misspelled plural nouns correctly.

21. Should we add oranges and blueberrys to the fruit salad?

_____

22. The girls made a chain of daisys for the visitors.

_____

© Loyola Press. Voyages in English   Grade 3

For additional help, review pages 34–35 in your textbook or visit www.voyagesinenglish.com.

2.5 Irregular Plural Nouns

The plurals of some nouns look somewhat different from their singular forms. These **irregular plurals** are not formed by adding -s or -es to the singular forms.

Write whether each noun is *singular, plural,* or *both*.

1. ox _____
2. deer _____
3. child _____
4. gentlemen _____
5. geese _____
6. moose _____

Complete each sentence with the plural of the noun in parentheses.

7. The _____ want to buy the boat. (man)

8. We watched the _____ swim in the pond. (goose)

9. The farmers used _____ to pull carts. (ox)

10. These _____ are waiting for the cashier. (woman)

11. Her _____ are all girls. (child)

12. His _____ were too big for those shoes. (foot)

13. Five _____ are standing near the barn. (sheep)

14. A family of _____ lives in the attic. (mouse)

15. Remember to brush your _____ every day. (tooth)

16. The _____ walk silently through the meadow. (deer)

Write a sentence using the plural of each noun.

17. watch _____

18. tooth _____

19. bench _____

20. sheep _____

21. country _____

22. moose _____

For additional help, review pages 36–37 in your textbook or visit www.voyagesinenglish.com.

© Loyola Press. Voyages in English   Grade 3

Section 2 • 25

2.5 Irregular Plural Nouns

The plurals of some nouns look somewhat different from their singular forms. These **irregular plurals** are not formed by adding *-s* or *-es* to the singular forms.

Complete each sentence with the singular or plural form of the noun in parentheses.

1. Blake got a _____ for his birthday. (mouse)

2. Several _____ are grazing in the meadow. (deer)

3. That _____ has a loud quack. (goose)

4. How many _____ do you have? (tooth)

5. Two large _____ pull the heavy cart. (ox)

6. Those _____ are my aunts. (woman)

7. She gave each _____ a snack. (child)

8. Corina is four _____ tall. (foot)

9. This is the biggest _____ in the flock. (sheep)

10. A herd of _____ is blocking the road. (moose)

11. Paper was first invented by the _____. (Chinese)

Rewrite each sentence. Write each misspelled plural noun correctly.

12. Her childs are both soccer players.

_____

13. Derrick has two loose tooths.

_____

14. Several sheeps are resting under the trees.

_____

15. Oxes are very strong animals.

_____

© Loyola Press. Voyages in English   Grade 3

For additional help, review pages 36–37 in your textbook or visit www.voyagesinenglish.com.

2.6 Singular Possessive Nouns

The **possessive form** of a noun shows possession, or ownership. To form the **singular possessive,** which is ownership by one person or thing, add an apostrophe and the letter *s* (-*'s*) to a singular noun.

Complete each sentence with the singular possessive form of the noun in parentheses.

1. I visited _____ house. (Taylor)

2. The _____ painting is beautiful. (artist)

3. _____ story was very funny. (Mr. Watson)

4. My _____ tail is orange and white. (cat)

5. Have you heard the _____ latest CD? (band)

6. That blue truck is my _____ car. (neighbor)

7. Our _____ gym is being painted. (school)

8. The _____ main office is in Des Moines. (company)

Rewrite each group of words, using a singular possessive noun.

9. the legs of a caterpillar _____

10. the umbrella of Diana _____

11. the bone of the dog _____

12. the sunflowers of Mrs. Carlson _____

13. the coins of our grandfather _____

14. the office of the dentist _____

Rewrite each sentence. Use the possessive form of the underlined noun.

15. Andrew borrowed his <u>brother</u> skateboard.

_____

16. Annabelle went to her <u>friend</u> party.

_____

© Loyola Press. Voyages in English   Grade 3

For additional help, review pages 38–39 in your textbook or visit www.voyagesinenglish.com.

2.7 Plural Possessive Nouns

A **plural possessive** shows that more than one person owns something. To form the plural possessive of most nouns, first make the singular noun plural. Then add an apostrophe after the *s* of the plural form.

Complete the chart.

	SINGULAR	PLURAL	PLURAL POSSESSIVE	
1.	brother	_____	_____	bicycles
2.	musician	_____	_____	instruments
3.	Chang	_____	_____	cars
4.	visitor	_____	_____	passes
5.	bunny	_____	_____	carrots
6.	coach	_____	_____	whistles

Complete each sentence with the plural possessive form of the noun in parentheses.

7. The two _____ jackets are fuzzy. (girl)

8. All the _____ boots were covered with snow. (singer)

9. The baby _____ heads bobbed up and down. (swan)

10. Those _____ bikes are in the garage. (boy)

11. The _____ trunks are very long. (elephant)

12. Our _____ home is by a lake. (grandparent)

Rewrite each group of words, using a plural possessive noun.

13. the cheers of the fans _____

14. the novels of the authors _____

15. the mayors of the cities _____

16. the purses of the girls _____

17. the arguments of the attorneys _____

18. the feathers of the canaries _____

For additional help, review pages 40–41 in your textbook or visit www.voyagesinenglish.com.

© Loyola Press. Voyages in English   Grade 3

2.8 Irregular Plural Possessive Nouns

The plural forms of irregular nouns do not end in *s*. To form the **plural possessive of irregular nouns,** add an apostrophe and the letter *s* (*-'s*) to the plural form of the word.

Complete the chart.

SINGULAR	PLURAL	PLURAL POSSESSIVE	
1. foot	_____	_____	skin
2. mouse	_____	_____	tails
3. goose	_____	_____	feathers
4. sheep	_____	_____	wool
5. child	_____	_____	games
6. gentleman	_____	_____	coats

Complete each sentence with the plural possessive form of the noun in parentheses.

7. The farmer loosened the _____ yokes. (ox)

8. The water fountain is near the _____ restroom. (woman)

9. David cleans the _____ cages once a week. (mouse)

10. These _____ antlers are very big. (moose)

11. Your _____ enamel is quite strong. (tooth)

12. We followed the _____ tracks to the stream. (deer)

Rewrite each sentence. Write each plural possessive noun correctly.

13. All womens' coats are on sale today.

_____

14. Have you seen the childrens' blocks?

_____

15. The mices' nests are hard to find.

_____

For additional help, review pages 42–43 in your textbook or visit www.voyagesinenglish.com.

Section 2 • 29

© Loyola Press. Voyages in English   Grade 3

2.9 Collective Nouns

A noun that names a group of things is called a **collective noun.** A collective noun usually uses an action word that ends in *s* in the present tense.

Underline the collective noun in each sentence.

1. A swarm of bees buzzed over the honey.

2. Our class went on a field trip to the zoo.

3. A herd of sheep grazes on the hillside.

4. The police officer asked the crowd to step back.

5. Which baseball team is your favorite?

6. The audience clapped at the end of the play.

7. The group of hikers rested along the trail.

8. When does the music club meet?

Complete each sentence with a noun from the word box.

family	flock	army	litter	crew	pair

9. A _____ of violinists played a duet.

10. The ship's _____ prepares to set sail.

11. A _____ of colorful parrots flew overhead.

12. Our cat just had a _____ of kittens.

13. My _____ eats dinner together every night.

14. The soldiers in this _____ are well trained.

Write a sentence for each collective noun.

15. band _____

16. pack _____

17. team _____

© Loyola Press. Voyages in English Grade 3

For additional help, review pages 44–45 in your textbook or visit www.voyagesinenglish.com.

2.9 Collective Nouns

A noun that names a group of things is called a **collective noun.**
A collective noun usually uses an action word that ends in *s* in the
present tense.

Write a collective noun to describe each group.

1. _____ of musicians

2. _____ of people

3. _____ of wolves

4. _____ of students

5. _____ of socks

6. _____ of soldiers

7. _____ of bees

8. _____ of sheep

**Cross out the collective noun used incorrectly in each sentence. Then rewrite
the sentence, using an appropriate collective noun.**

9. Our herd went on a field trip to the farm.

_____

10. An army of kittens slept together in the pet bed.

_____

11. Uncle Scott raises a team of sheep.

_____

12. The mayor addressed the family of reporters.

_____

13. The swarm cheered and chanted for an encore.

_____

© Loyola Press. Voyages in English   Grade 3

For additional help, review pages 44–45 in your textbook
or visit www.voyagesinenglish.com.

Section 2 • 31

2.10 Nouns as Subjects

A **noun** may be used as the subject of a sentence. The subject tells what the sentence is about. It tells who or what does something.

Underline the noun used as the subject in each sentence.

1. Eduardo looked very excited.

2. The nest is on the lowest branch.

3. Vitamins come in all shapes and colors.

4. The eggs are in the basket.

5. Lisa has soccer practice twice a week.

6. The octopus swims over the coral.

7. Many fans attended the concert.

8. Ethan will write his report tonight.

9. The pilot prepares for takeoff.

Complete each sentence with a subject from the word box.

| team | buzzer | Andy | fans | Coach Smith |

10. _____ spoke to his basketball players.

11. The _____ had one chance to win the game.

12. _____ shot the ball through the hoop.

13. The final _____ sounded.

14. The excited _____ in the stands cheered.

Write a sentence for each topic. Underline each subject.

15. a favorite sport _____

16. a place to relax _____

17. a friend _____

© Loyola Press. Voyages in English   Grade 3

For additional help, review pages 46–47 in your textbook or visit www.voyagesinenglish.com.

2.11 Words Used as Nouns *and* as Verbs

Many words can be used both as nouns and as verbs. Check closely to see how a word is used in a specific sentence.

Write whether each underlined word is used as a *noun* or as a *verb*.

1. Put another <u>stick</u> on the fire. _____

2. The glue will <u>stick</u> to the cloth. _____

3. Does your dog <u>bark</u> all the time? _____

4. We can study the <u>bark</u> on the tree. _____

5. John will <u>blaze</u> a trail for us. _____

6. The <u>blaze</u> was put out by the firefighters. _____

7. Please put the <u>brush</u> in the drawer. _____

8. <u>Brush</u> your teeth after every meal. _____

9. Kate <u>files</u> charts for the doctor. _____

10. Which <u>files</u> did you need me to find? _____

Write *swim*, *star*, and *serve* twice to complete the sentences. Write whether each word is used as a *noun* or as a *verb*.

11. Do you see that _____ in the sky? _____

12. My sisters _____ in the play. _____

13. Let's go for a _____ in the lake. _____

14. I _____ in my friend's pool. _____

15. Would you _____ me more peas? _____

16. I must practice my tennis _____. _____

Write two sentences using *light*, once as a noun and once as a verb. Then write how you used the word in each sentence.

17. _____

18. _____

© Loyola Press. Voyages in English   Grade 3

For additional help, review pages 48–49 in your textbook or visit www.voyagesinenglish.com.

Section 2 • 33

SECTION 3 Daily Maintenance

3.1 **The hungry frog catches flies.**

    1. Which word is a plural noun?   _____

    2. Is this plural noun regular or irregular?   _____

    3. Is *frog* a common noun or a proper noun?   _____

    4. Diagram the sentence here.

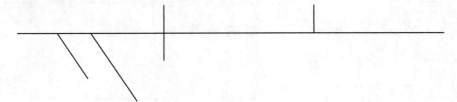

3.2 **Susan's sister gives piano lessons.**

    1. Which word is a possessive noun?   _____

    2. Is this word singular or plural?   _____

    3. Is the sentence a statement or a command?   _____

    4. Diagram the sentence here.

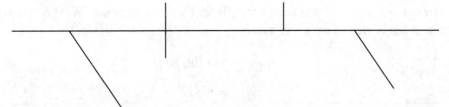

3.3 **The young children draw pictures.**

    1. What is the complete subject?   _____

    2. What is the simple predicate?   _____

    3. Which word is an irregular plural noun?   _____

    4. Diagram the sentence here.

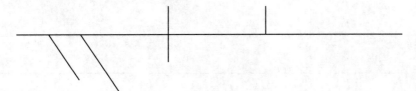

© Loyola Press. Voyages in English   **Grade 3**

3.4 **I like the girls' pink dresses.**

1. Is the pronoun singular or plural?   _____

2. Which word is a possessive noun?   _____

3. Is the possessive noun singular or plural?   _____

4. Diagram the sentence here.

3.5 **Marc and Jared play basketball.**

1. Is the subject or the predicate compound?   _____

2. Which words are proper nouns?   _____

3. Is the verb present tense or past tense?   _____

4. Diagram the sentence here.

3.6 **We cleaned the mice's cages.**

1. What is the subject pronoun?   _____

2. What is the simple predicate?   _____

3. Which word is a plural possessive noun?   _____

4. Diagram the sentence here.

© Loyola Press. Voyages in English   Grade 3

3.7 **The band played five songs.**

1. What kind of sentence is this? _____

2. Which word is a collective noun? _____

3. Which word describes *songs*? _____

4. Diagram the sentence here.

3.8 **Emilio makes delicious tacos.**

1. Which noun is the subject of the sentence? _____

2. Is the verb present tense or past tense? _____

3. Which word is a common noun? _____

4. Diagram the sentence here.

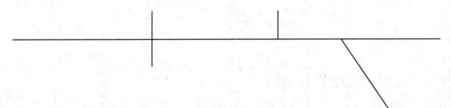

© Loyola Press. Voyages in English Grade 3

3.1 Pronouns

A **pronoun** is a word that takes the place of a noun. A **personal pronoun** refers to the person who is speaking or to the person or thing that is spoken to or about.

Underline the personal pronoun or pronouns in each sentence.

1. Do you like spaghetti and meatballs?

2. They are players on the team.

3. She threw it away.

4. Watch them do the latest dance.

5. I hope we can go to the zoo tomorrow.

6. He lost it in the sand.

7. I helped him carry the groceries.

8. Where did they go on vacation?

9. Jeff gave us money for the movie.

10. We think they are very funny.

Write a personal pronoun to take the place of the underlined word or words in each sentence.

11. Adam and I went to the train museum. _____

12. The students want to learn more about volcanoes. _____

13. The neighbors are painting their house. _____

14. Ms. Garcia asked Trent to stay after class. _____

15. The raccoon knocked over the trash cans. _____

16. Ray, Brian, and Fernando play soccer. _____

Write a sentence that includes at least one noun. Then rewrite the sentence, using a pronoun to replace each noun.

17. _____

_____

© Loyola Press. Voyages in English   Grade 3

For additional help, review pages 54–55 in your textbook or visit www.voyagesinenglish.com.

3.2 Subject Pronouns

Some personal pronouns may be used as the subject of a sentence. These are called **subject pronouns.** The subject pronouns are *I, you, he, she, it, we,* and *they.*

Underline the subject pronoun in each sentence.

1. I want to go to the beach.

2. It looks good on Leah.

3. She asked Michelle to play checkers.

4. We play catch on the baseball field.

5. Later she made popcorn.

6. They rested after their long hike.

7. It has pretty pink blossoms.

Write a subject pronoun to take the place of the underlined word or words in each sentence.

8. The Petersons organized the block party.   _____

9. Steve cooked hamburgers on the grill.   _____

10. Margie and I made potato salad.   _____

11. The food was delicious.   _____

12. Mrs. Nguyen brought her two poodles.   _____

13. The dogs playfully chased the children.   _____

14. Loretta sang and played her guitar.   _____

15. The block party was a success.   _____

Write a subject pronoun that completes each sentence. Use a clue in the sentence for help.

16. _____ bought red shoes to match her dress.

17. _____ signed my name at the bottom of the letter.

18. _____ is visiting his brother in Atlanta.

For additional help, review pages 56–57 in your textbook or visit www.voyagesinenglish.com.

© Loyola Press. Voyages in English   Grade 3

3.3 Object Pronouns

Some pronouns may be used after an action verb in a sentence. These are called **object pronouns.** The object pronouns are *me, you, him, her, it, us,* and *them.*

Underline the object pronoun in each sentence.

1. Henry showed me his boat.

2. Dad drove it around the lake.

3. Silvia asked her for a towel.

4. Tell him to go faster.

5. Kim and Bill invited us to go waterskiing.

6. We want them to bring the skis and life jackets.

7. I told you about the canoe rentals.

Circle the pronoun or pronouns that complete each sentence.

8. Mario saw (she   her) at the fair on Saturday.

9. Claire bought (I   me) a book about the solar system.

10. Mrs. Anderson taught (us   we) two new songs.

11. We joined (them   they) for dinner after the movie.

12. Coach Sanders chose (her   she) and (me   I) for the team.

13. Scott asked (me   I) to help (he   him) with a math problem.

Write an object pronoun to take the place of the underlined word or words in each sentence.

14. Frank left his science report at home.   _____

15. Please give Mike the music magazine.   _____

16. We invited Eddie and Arlene to the concert.   _____

17. The crowd enjoyed the halftime show.   _____

18. Call Peter and me when you are ready to go.   _____

19. I will visit my cousin Vanessa next week.   _____

© Loyola Press. Voyages in English   Grade 3

For additional help, review pages 58–59 in your textbook or visit www.voyagesinenglish.com.

3.3 Object Pronouns

Some personal pronouns may be used after an action verb in a sentence. These are called **object pronouns.** The object pronouns are *me, you, him, her, it, us,* and *them.*

Circle the correct object pronoun or pronouns that complete each sentence.

1. Greg sent (she   her) a thank-you note.

2. Please give (us   we) our allowance for the week.

3. Sandra will send (them   they) an invitation.

4. The coach told (he   him) to run another lap.

5. I bought (they   it) at the swap meet.

6. We saw (she   you) at the skate park on Friday night.

7. Kate showed (him   he) and (we   us) pictures of her new puppy.

8. The loud crash in the kitchen startled (I   me) and (her   she).

Rewrite each sentence. Use correct object pronouns.

9. Dr. Adams told she about the operation.

_____

10. We want he on our softball team.

_____

11. They asked I and he to bring the snacks.

_____

12. You sent they the wrong item.

_____

13. He will give we five dollars for this chair.

_____

14. They drove I and she to school this morning.

© Loyola Press. Voyages in English **Grade 3**

For additional help, review pages 58–59 in your textbook or visit www.voyagesinenglish.com.

3.4 Possessive Pronouns

A **possessive pronoun** shows who or what owns something. A possessive pronoun takes the place of both the person who owns the thing and the object that is owned.

Underline the possessive pronoun or pronouns in each sentence.

1. Mine is an iguana.

2. Yours is smaller than my guinea pig.

3. She is holding hers on a towel.

4. I patted his on the head.

5. Theirs are chasing a tennis ball.

6. What do you feed yours?

7. Ours sleeps during the day and is awake at night.

8. His is playing with mine.

Write the letter of the possessive pronoun in Column B that replaces the words in Column A.

COLUMN A		COLUMN B	
9. Brynn's and Kai's kites	_____	a.	hers
10. Wendy's bat	_____	b.	yours
11. my baseball glove	_____	c.	theirs
12. your bike helmet	_____	d.	his
13. his skateboard	_____	e.	ours
14. our soccer cleats	_____	f.	mine

Write a possessive pronoun to replace the underlined words in each sentence.

15. Your painting is very colorful.   _____

16. My photo is on the back wall.   _____

17. My drawing and Sam's drawing got second prize.   _____

18. The blue ribbon went to Carl and Ryan's statue. _____

© Loyola Press. Voyages in English   Grade 3

For additional help, review pages 60–61 in your textbook or visit www.voyagesinenglish.com.

3.5 Possessive Adjectives

Possessive adjectives are adjectives that come before nouns to show ownership. The possessive adjectives are *my, your, his, her, its, our,* and *their.* Do not confuse possessive pronouns and possessive adjectives.

Underline the possessive adjective in each sentence.

1. Marie cannot find her blue shirt.

2. The boys ride their bicycles to the park.

3. Nate plays with his new basketball.

4. Our parents are both teachers.

5. May I borrow your baseball glove?

6. Its paws are covered with mud.

7. My hair is short and curly.

8. Have you heard their latest song?

Underline each possessive pronoun and circle each possessive adjective.

9. These marbles are his.

10. His older brother is very tall.

11. Mine is the last house on the left.

12. Did you like her poem?

13. Your parents must complete and return this form.

14. We do not ride our bikes to school.

15. My hair is longer than hers.

16. Their backyard looks a lot like mine.

Write two sentences that tell about you and a friend. Use a possessive adjective in one sentence and a possessive pronoun in the other sentence.

17. _____

18. _____

© Loyola Press. Voyages in English   Grade 3

For additional help, review pages 62–63 in your textbook or visit www.voyagesinenglish.com.

3.6 Agreement of Pronouns and Verbs

A subject and its verb must agree. A verb that shows an action is often in the present tense. Most subjects take the same form of the verb in the present tense.

Circle the verb that agrees with the subject pronoun to complete each sentence.

1. He (hold   holds) the picnic basket.

2. She (watch   watches) a hummingbird.

3. They (chase   chases) a butterfly.

4. We (feed   feeds) the pigeons in the park.

5. It (rest   rests) under a tree.

6. I (walk   walks) along the path.

7. We (pick   picks) pretty pink flowers.

8. They (sit   sits) on a wooden bench.

Write the correct form of the verb in parentheses to complete each sentence.

9. She _____ across the pool. (swim)

10. I _____ singing with my sister. (practice)

11. He _____ the ball over the fence. (hit)

12. You _____ the ball in your glove. (catch)

13. It _____ a lot of attention. (needs)

14. I _____ the ball through the hoop. (shoot)

15. They _____ new boots. (buy)

16. We _____ for the home team. (cheer)

Write a sentence for each subject pronoun, using the correct verb form.

17. He _____

18. It _____

© Loyola Press. Voyages in English   Grade 3

For additional help, review pages 63–64 in your textbook or visit www.voyagesinenglish.com.

3.6 Agreement of Pronouns and Verbs

A subject and its verb must agree. A verb that shows an action is often in the present tense. Most subjects take the same form of the verb in the present tense.

Write a subject pronoun to complete each sentence.

1. We _____ in the school choir. (sing)

2. He _____ stories about superheroes. (write)

3. I _____ empty cans and bottles. (recycle)

4. They _____ piano lessons on Monday afternoon. (take)

5. She _____ each guest at the front door. (greet)

6. You _____ at the silliest things. (laugh)

Rewrite each sentence. Make sure the subject pronoun and the verb agree.

7. It catch the ball in its mouth.

_____

8. She give the dog a bowl of water.

_____

9. They wants more time to finish the assignment.

_____

10. You works harder than the other players.

_____

On another sheet of paper, match each pronoun with a verb. Write a sentence with each pair, using the pronoun as the subject.

PRONOUNS	VERBS
she you I it	talk sleep eat explore

© Loyola Press. Voyages in English   Grade 3

For additional help, review pages 64–65 in your textbook or visit www.voyagesinenglish.com.

3.7 *I and Me*

> *I* and *me* are used when you talk about yourself. *I* is used as the subject of a sentence. *Me* is used as an object.

Circle the correct pronoun to complete each sentence.

1. (I   me) need a new umbrella.

2. (I   me) cannot lift this large box.

3. On weekends (I   me) sleep late.

4. Sheila showed (I   me) her charm bracelet.

5. On Saturday Dad drove (I   me) to my dance class.

6. For a treat (I   me) made fruit smoothies.

7. Please help (I   me) wash the car.

8. Can you teach (I   me) that card trick?

Write *I* or *me* to complete each sentence.

9. Dad thanked _____ for my help.

10. _____ earned two dollars for walking the dog.

11. Watch _____ on the slide.

12. Yes, _____ made the chicken soup.

13. Aunt Elaine invited _____ to the boat show.

14. My sister told _____ about her tryouts for the play.

Circle the pronoun that completes each sentence. Then write whether each pronoun is a *subject pronoun* or an *object pronoun*.

15. Kris gave (I   me) two movie passes. _____

16. (I   me) like going to the aquarium. _____

17. Mom asked (I   me) to take out the trash. _____

18. Gary and (I   me) take swimming lessons. _____

19. Dylan told (I   me) about the dinosaur exhibit. _____

© Loyola Press. Voyages in English   Grade 3

For additional help, review pages 66–67 in your textbook or visit www.voyagesinenglish.com.

3.8 Compound Subjects and Objects

Pronouns can be used in compound subjects and compound objects. Use a subject pronoun in a compound subject. Use an object pronoun in a compound object.

Underline the compound subject or compound object in each sentence.

1. She and Lauren are making friendship bracelets.

2. The judges awarded him and her the top prize.

3. Ismael invited Jake and us to play a game.

4. Patty and he are talented clarinet players.

5. They and we attended the book fair on Tuesday night.

Circle the subject pronoun or pronouns that complete each sentence.

6. Alicia and (I   me) walked to the library.

7. Brad and (he   him) are best friends.

8. Dora and (they   them) cleaned up their rooms.

9. (Her   She) and Dad drove to the store.

10. (Us   We) and the neighbors put out the trash on Monday.

11. (He   Him) and (I   me) organized the books on the shelves.

12. (They   Them) and (us   we) were pleased with the decision.

Circle the object pronoun or pronouns that complete each sentence.

13. Stacy made Frank and (us   we) pancakes for breakfast.

14. Vicky wants Mike and (I   me) to sing a song.

15. The teacher allowed Tracy and (him   he) to finish their report later.

16. Will pushed Jana and (me   I) on the swings.

17. Nina showed (they   them) and (she   her) the kittens.

18. We took (he   him) and (her   she) back home.

19. Mr. Walters showed (him   he) and (us   we) how to add three numbers.

© Loyola Press. Voyages in English   Grade 3

For additional help, review pages 68–69 in your textbook or visit www.voyagesinenglish.com.

SECTION 4 Daily Maintenance

4.1 **She takes ballet lessons.**

1. Is *She* a noun or a pronoun?   _____

2. What is the verb?   _____

3. Which word describes *lessons*?   _____

4. Diagram the sentence here.

4.2 **We plant pumpkin seeds.**

1. What is the subject pronoun?   _____

2. What is the verb?   _____

3. What is the plural noun?   _____

4. Diagram the sentence here.

4.3 **The feather tickles me.**

1. Is the subject simple or compound?   _____

2. What is the verb?   _____

3. What is the object pronoun?   _____

4. Diagram the sentence here.

© Loyola Press. Voyages in English Grade 3

4.4 **My brother is a surfer.**

1. Is the subject simple or compound? _____

2. What is the verb? _____

3. What is the possessive adjective? _____

4. Diagram the sentence here.

4.5 **Hers is the pink backpack.**

1. What is the possessive pronoun? _____

2. What is the verb? _____

3. Is the verb an action verb or a being verb? _____

4. Diagram the sentence here.

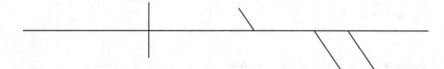

4.6 **Tina found her keys.**

1. What is the proper noun? _____

2. What is the verb? _____

3. What is the direct object? _____

4. Diagram the sentence here.

© Loyola Press. Voyages in English   Grade 3

4.7 **Our neighbors are friendly.**

1. What is the plural noun? _____

2. What is the verb? _____

3. Which word is a possessive adjective? _____

4. Diagram the sentence here.

4.8 **The volcano amazed him.**

1. What is the complete subject? _____

2. What is the complete predicate? _____

3. What is the object pronoun? _____

4. Diagram the sentence here.

4.9 **The girls play hopscotch.**

1. Is the sentence a statement or a command? _____

2. Is *girls* a noun or a pronoun? _____

3. Is *play* used as a noun or as a verb? _____

4. Diagram the sentence here.

© Loyola Press. Voyages in English   Grade 3

4.10 **I made the chicken tacos.**

1. What is the simple subject?   _____

2. What is the simple predicate?   _____

3. Is the pronoun singular or plural?   _____

4. Diagram the sentence here.

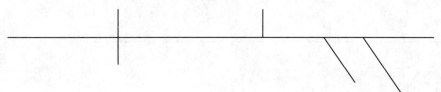

4.11 **The librarian helped me.**

1. Is the subject a noun or a pronoun?   _____

2. What is the verb?   _____

3. What is the object pronoun?   _____

4. Diagram the sentence here.

4.12 **They like his scooter.**

1. What is the subject?   _____

2. What is the verb?   _____

3. Which word is a possessive adjective?   _____

4. Diagram the sentence here.

© Loyola Press. Voyages in English   Grade 3

4.13 **Mine is the orange cat.**

1. Is the subject a noun or a pronoun?   _____

2. Which word is a common noun?   _____

3. Which word is an adjective?   _____

4. Diagram the sentence here.

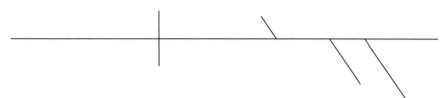

4.14 **He cleaned his room.**

1. What is the complete subject?   _____

2. What is the complete predicate?   _____

3. Is *He* a noun or a pronoun?   _____

4. Diagram the sentence here.

4.15 **Lily is their sister.**

1. What is the common noun?   _____

2. What is the verb?   _____

3. What is the subject complement?   _____

4. Diagram the sentence here.

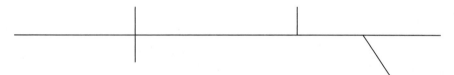

© Loyola Press. Voyages in English   Grade 3

4.16 **I juggled three balls.**

1. Is *three* a noun or an adjective?   _____

2. Is *juggled* the subject or the verb?   _____

3. Is *I* a pronoun or a noun?   _____

4. Diagram the sentence here.

© Loyola Press. Voyages in English   Grade 3

4.1 Action Verbs

Many verbs express action. An **action verb** tells what someone or something does.

Underline the action verb in each sentence.

1. Steve and Esai play in the school band.

2. They sit in the brass section.

3. Esai holds his trumpet.

4. Steve carries his heavy tuba.

5. Mr. Samson claps the beat of the music.

6. Music fills the crowded band room.

7. The musicians tap their feet.

8. They practice each song several times.

Use an action verb from the word box to complete each sentence.

reads	sits	walk	looks	writes	use	helps	talk

9. Cornell and Shannon _____ to the library.

10. Cornell _____ a book report.

11. Shannon _____ for a book about bears.

12. The librarian _____ Shannon find a book.

13. Several students _____ quietly in the corner.

14. Ms. Peters _____ near the magazines.

15. Some people _____ the computers.

16. A woman _____ a book to a young boy.

Write a sentence using each action verb.

17. eat _____

18. pretend _____

© Loyola Press. Voyages in English   Grade 3

For additional help, review pages 74–75 in your textbook
or visit www.voyagesinenglish.com.

Section 4 • 53

4.2   Being Verbs

> A **being verb** shows what someone or something is. Being verbs do not express action.

Underline the being verb in each sentence.

1. My family is very large.

2. Maria and John are sick today.

3. The stars are bright tonight.

4. He has been on the phone a long time.

5. We were tired after the long walk home.

6. I am the captain of my soccer team.

7. Our cousins will be here tomorrow.

8. They had been waiting for an hour.

Circle the being verb that correctly completes each sentence.

9. My chicken soup (are   is) cold.

10. Mikaela (was   were) late again.

11. Nicole's hamsters (are   am) small and fluffy.

12. Someday I (will be   have been) a grown-up.

13. We (was   were) ready for the spelling test.

14. Lisa (have been   has been) to my house before.

Underline the verb in each sentence. Write whether the verb is an *action verb* or a *being verb*.

15. My brother is very happy today.   _____

16. That math problem was difficult.   _____

17. The bus driver waits for the passengers.   _____

18. The children are excited about the party.   _____

19. I am the youngest person in my family.   _____

© Loyola Press. Voyages in English   Grade 3

For additional help, review pages 76–77 in your textbook or visit www.voyagesinenglish.com.

4.2   Being Verbs

A **being verb** shows what someone or something is. Being verbs do not express action.

Underline the verb in each sentence. Write whether the verb is an *action verb* or a *being verb*.

1. My hands are cold today.   _____

2. The dog chased a small red ball.   _____

3. Tina was at the football game tonight.   _____

4. The kittens were in a basket.   _____

5. Pete chose a book about trains.   _____

6. I had been sick all week.   _____

Use a being verb from the word box to complete each sentence.

was   will be   are   have been   is   am   has been   were

7. I _____ nine years old.

8. Mother _____ home in 10 minutes.

9. The students _____ at school all day.

10. Joanna _____ late for class yesterday.

11. Ezekiel _____ now ready for his oral report.

12. Those boys _____ in my class last year.

13. She _____ at every game this season.

14. They _____ to our house many times.

Write a sentence using each verb.

15. am _____

16. was _____

17. has been _____

© Loyola Press. Voyages in English   Grade 3

For additional help, review pages 76–77 in your textbook or visit www.voyagesinenglish.com.

4.3 Helping Verbs

A verb can have more than one word. A **helping verb** is a verb added before a main verb to make the meaning clear.

Underline the helping verb in each sentence.

1. I am taking piano lessons.

2. She might join our club.

3. They have planted vegetables in the garden.

4. We can attend the concert.

5. Amir will perform with us.

6. He had planned to take the bus.

7. Josh and I were practicing our song.

8. Irina does want another glass of water.

Underline the helping verb once and the main verb twice in each sentence.

9. She might win the race.

10. I can solve the last problem.

11. The children are waiting on the playground.

12. A police officer will patrol the streets.

13. Dina did complete her work on time.

14. They have mailed the invitations.

15. Debby and Javier were shopping for a new game.

Circle the helping verb that correctly completes each sentence.

16. I (is   am) talking on the phone.

17. They (might   are) returning their library books.

18. Nicolas (has   have) planned a camping trip.

19. We (can   is) help you carry the bags.

20. Chris and Mike (do   does) want to go with us.

© Loyola Press. Voyages in English   **Grade 3**

For additional help, review pages 78–79 in your textbook or visit www.voyagesinenglish.com.

4.3 Helping Verbs

A verb can have more than one word. A **helping verb** is a verb added before a main verb to make the meaning clear.

Underline the helping verb once and the main verb twice in each sentence.

1. The play will begin in 15 minutes.
2. I can see the mountains from my backyard.
3. We had stayed there last summer.
4. Mr. Andrews did work at the hospital.
5. Wyatt and Ken might play a video game.
6. Mrs. Lee is driving the school bus today.

Write a verb from the word box to complete each sentence.

will	were	do	is	have	am

7. I _____ washing the dishes in the sink.
8. Maddy and Melanie _____ like the spicy noodles.
9. The movie _____ end at noon.
10. We _____ visited this beach before.
11. Dean _____ fixing his bicycle.
12. Our dogs _____ barking last night.

Rewrite each sentence. Use the correct helping verb.

13. We is going there this weekend.

_____

14. I does see you tomorrow.

_____

15. Chris have gone to the store.

_____

© Loyola Press. Voyages in English Grade 3

For additional help, review pages 78–79 in your textbook or visit www.voyagesinenglish.com.

4.4 Principal Parts of Verbs

A verb has four principal parts: **present, present participle, past,** and **past participle.**

Write whether the underlined word in each sentence is *present or past*.

1. This artist <u>makes</u> beautiful drawings. _____
2. Trisha <u>walked</u> to the park. _____
3. Bill and Jin <u>study</u> together. _____
4. She <u>mailed</u> the package. _____
5. The clerk <u>counted</u> the money. _____

Write whether the underlined word in each sentence is *present participle* or *past participle*.

6. I am <u>learning</u> Spanish from my father. _____
7. I have <u>visited</u> her several times this month. _____
8. They are <u>raising</u> money for our school. _____
9. Maya was <u>cleaning</u> her room. _____
10. He had <u>finished</u> the book in just one week. _____

Complete each sentence with the form of the verb in parentheses.

11. The plumber is _____ the leak. (fix—present participle)
12. Mr. Neilson has _____ me before. (coach—past participle)
13. Paula _____ her own dresses. (sew—present)
14. I _____ my homework. (finish—past)
15. Darius _____ in his father's office. (help—present)
16. The players are _____ across the field. (run—present participle)
17. The shoppers _____ into the store. (rush—past)
18. Jimmy always _____ a turkey sandwich. (order—present)
19. Everyone _____ the clowns in the center ring. (watch—past)

© Loyola Press. Voyages in English Grade 3

For additional help, review pages 80–81 in your textbook or visit www.voyagesinenglish.com.

4.4 Principal Parts of Verbs

A verb has four principal parts: **present, present participle, past,** and **past participle.**

Complete the chart with the correct form of each verb.

PRESENT	PRESENT PARTICIPLE	PAST	PAST PARTICIPLE
1. cook	_____	_____	_____
2. point	_____	_____	_____
3. smile	_____	_____	_____
4. brush	_____	_____	_____
5. call	_____	_____	_____
6. learn	_____	_____	_____

Complete each sentence with a verb. Use the form in parentheses.

7. The students are _____ outside. (present participle)

8. He _____ his project last night. (past)

9. The judges _____ our group's performance. (past)

10. She is _____ at the mall. (present participle)

11. Dad had _____ the package yesterday. (past participle)

12. The players _____ after school. (present)

Rewrite each sentence correctly. Use the correct verb.

13. The boy is waited for his mother.

_____

14. Ms. Jones have helped me with my homework.

_____

15. Cesar walking to school every day.

_____

For additional help, review pages 80–81 in your textbook or visit www.voyagesinenglish.com.

Section 4 • 59

© Loyola Press. Voyages in English   Grade 3

4.5 Regular and Irregular Verbs

The past and the past participle of **regular verbs** usually end in -*d* or -*ed*. The past and the past participle of **irregular verbs** are not formed by adding -*d* or -*ed* to the present.

Complete the chart with the correct parts of the verbs.

	PRESENT	PRESENT PARTICIPLE	PAST	PAST PARTICIPLE
1.	give	_____	_____	_____
2.	_____	flying	_____	_____
3.	_____	_____	_____	begun
4.	put	_____	_____	_____
5.	_____	_____	_____	sung
6.	_____	_____	did	_____

Write whether each underlined verb is *regular* or *irregular*.

7. Cathy <u>sang</u> her favorite song.   _____

8. Andre and I <u>painted</u> the chairs blue.   _____

9. The baby bird <u>flew</u> from the nest.   _____

10. The doctor <u>helped</u> the sick boy.   _____

11. Our class <u>wrote</u> a letter to students in Mexico.   _____

12. Who <u>told</u> you about this restaurant?   _____

13. We <u>laughed</u> at Sally's silly joke.   _____

Circle the word that correctly completes each sentence.

14. I (felled   felt) the earthquake yesterday.

15. She (put   putted) the coin in her pocket.

16. We (rided   rode) in a taxi to get to the airport.

17. Wesley (throwed   threw) the ball to Kyle.

18. The boy (tripped   tript) over his shoelace.

© Loyola Press. Voyages in English   Grade 3

For additional help, review pages 82–83 in your textbook or visit www.voyagesinenglish.com.

4.6 *Bring, Buy, Come, and Sit*

Bring, buy, come, and sit are irregular verbs. You must learn how to form each part of these verbs correctly. Remember that the present participle and the past participle are often used with helping verbs.

Underline the part of *bring, buy, come,* or *sit* in each sentence. Then write whether the part is *present, present participle, past,* or *past participle*.

1. The painter is coming tomorrow. _____

2. We bought corn at the farmers' market. _____

3. He has brought snacks for movie night. _____

4. The fans sit in the bleachers. _____

5. Joel came to see us last week. _____

6. The children are sitting on the couch. _____

Circle the verb that correctly completes each sentence.

7. Arturo is (bringing   brought) my glasses.

8. The guide (brought   bring) water for the hike.

9. Richard (buy   bought) the poster for his dad.

10. Mrs. Patel was (bought   buying) a toy for the baby.

11. Josie has (come   came) to see each new band.

12. Who is (come   coming) to the game tonight?

13. Mr. Briggs had (sit   sat) for a while to rest.

14. I am (sat   sitting) with my best friend.

Complete each sentence with the correct part of the verb in parentheses.

15. My dog is _____ next to hers. (sit)

16. She had _____ corn tortillas last week. (buy)

17. A package _____ for you yesterday. (come)

18. Clarice had _____ flowers for me. (bring)

19. My friends are _____ here for a sleepover. (come)

© Loyola Press. Voyages in English   Grade 3

For additional help, review pages 84–85 in your textbook or visit www.voyagesinenglish.com.

4.7 *Eat, Go, and See*

> *Eat, go,* and *see* are irregular verbs. You must learn how to form each part of these verbs correctly. Remember that the present participle and the past participle are often used with helping verbs.

Circle the verb that correctly completes each sentence.

1. We (ate   eat) shrimp for dinner.

2. They have (saw   seen) us in town many times.

3. I (went   gone) to the dentist yesterday.

4. Teresa had (went   gone) to this market before.

5. Who has (eat   eaten) all the apples?

6. He (see   sees) many runners during his morning walk.

7. Mika is (going   gone) to the hobby shop with me.

Complete each sentence with the correct part of the verb in parentheses.

8. She often _____ lunch at that shop. (eat)

9. He has _____ there several times. (go)

10. Carrie _____ a shooting star last night. (see)

11. We are _____ the watermelon slices. (eat)

12. Roger and I _____ to a baseball game. (go)

13. Who _____ my toast? (eat)

14. We have _____ many deer on this trail. (see)

15. They are _____ to the skate park with us. (go)

Write a sentence using each verb in the form shown in parentheses.

16. go (past) _____

17. see (past participle) _____

18. eat (present) _____

19. go (present participle) _____

© Loyola Press. Voyages in English   Grade 3

For additional help, review pages 86–87 in your textbook or visit www.voyagesinenglish.com.

4.8 Take, Tear, and Write

Take, tear, and write are irregular verbs. You must learn how to form each part of these verbs correctly. Remember that the present participle and the past participle are often used with helping verbs.

Circle the verb that correctly completes each sentence.

1. Henry (take   takes) skiing lessons.

2. I (tore   torn) a hole in my shirt.

3. Charlie has (wrote   written) a good personal narrative.

4. We are (wrote   writing) a letter to our grandfather.

5. Sammy (took   taken) me to the post office.

6. The puppy has (tore   torn) its blanket.

7. I am (take   taking) a dance class on Monday night.

Complete each sentence with the correct part of the verb in parentheses.

8. Jill always _____ her name with a pink pen. (write)

9. The strap of my backpack has _____. (tear)

10. Last summer we _____ our friends to the lake. (take)

11. She has _____ a funny poem. (write)

12. Brad is _____ her to the airport at noon. (take)

13. I _____ the paper into strips. (tear)

Underline the verb in each sentence. Then write whether the verb is _present_, _present participle_, _past_, or _past participle_.

14. We write letters to our pen pals in Germany.   _____

15. I have taken a music class before.   _____

16. She tore her jacket on that fence.   _____

17. He wrote his name on his paper.   _____

18. Shawn took Fluffy to the vet.   _____

19. Mom is tearing the coupons from the booklet.   _____

© Loyola Press. Voyages in English   Grade 3

For additional help, review pages 88–89 in your textbook
or visit www.voyagesinenglish.com.

4.9   Simple Present Tense

A verb in the **simple present tense** tells about something that is always true or an action that happens again and again.

Circle the verb that correctly completes each sentence.

1. My parents (plant   plants) a garden every year.

2. My mother (like   likes) flowers.

3. She (start   starts) many kinds of seeds.

4. They (bloom   blooms) all summer long.

5. My father (grow   grows) wonderful vegetables.

6. His tomatoes (taste   tastes) great.

7. The birds sometimes (get   gets) to them first.

8. We (help   helps) in the garden too.

Write whether the underlined subject in each sentence is *singular* or *plural*. Then circle the verb that correctly completes the sentence.

9. A bee (fly   flies) above the flowers.   _____

10. Brown leaves (fall   falls) from the trees.   _____

11. Squirrels (look   looks) for nuts.   _____

12. Dandelions (move   moves) in the wind.   _____

13. The sun (shine   shines) on the garden.   _____

14. Sara (pull   pulls) weeds from the ground.   _____

15. Worms (wiggle   wiggles) in the dirt.   _____

16. A hungry bird (catch   catches) a worm.   _____

Write a sentence for each subject. Use a verb in the simple present tense.

17. car _____

18. brother _____

19. dancers _____

© Loyola Press. Voyages in English   Grade 3

For additional help, review pages 90–91 in your textbook or visit www.voyagesinenglish.com.

4.10 Simple Past Tense

A verb in the **simple past tense** tells about something that happened in the past.

Write the simple past tense of each verb.

1. learn _____
2. save _____
3. go _____
4. make _____
5. laugh _____
6. ride _____

7. bake _____
8. eat _____
9. sing _____
10. carry _____
11. buy _____
12. reply _____

Complete each sentence with the simple past tense of the verb in parentheses.

13. I _____ the bucket with fresh water. (fill)

14. Mrs. Jenkins _____ our homework. (collect)

15. He _____ proud of his painting. (feel)

16. Ali _____ in the talent show with me. (perform)

17. We _____ to the store to buy milk. (drive)

18. Who _____ you that large package? (send)

19. The audience _____ at the end of the play. (clap)

20. Eli _____ the button for the elevator. (push)

21. Everyone _____ to the bus stop. (hurry)

Rewrite each sentence. Change the verb to the simple past tense.

22. Evan listens to music on his headphones.

_____

23. The movie begins after lunch.

_____

© Loyola Press. Voyages in English   Grade 3

For additional help, review pages 92–93 in your textbook or visit www.voyagesinenglish.com.

4.11 Future Tense with *Will*

> The word *will* is one way to express something that will take place in the future. The helping verb *will* is used with the present part of a verb to form a future tense.

Complete each sentence with the verb in parentheses. Use the future tense with *will*.

1. Tim _____ his paragraph. (revise)

2. Many parents _____ Back-to-School Night. (attend)

3. We _____ these cans and bottles. (recycle)

4. I _____ this money on a new CD. (spend)

5. The concert _____ in five minutes. (begin)

Rewrite each sentence. Change the verb to the future tense with *will*.

6. Charla makes the salad.

   _____

7. I prepare the chicken kabobs.

   _____

8. Dirk cleans the patio.

   _____

Underline the verb in each sentence. Write whether the tense of the verb is *simple present*, *simple past*, or *future*.

9. I will walk the dog today. _____

10. Your new puppy is very playful. _____

11. My sister will repair the broken mug. _____

12. Our neighbors sent us a postcard from Hawaii. _____

13. Eddie's father teaches a computer class. _____

14. Joey hit the ball straight to the pitcher. _____

For additional help, review pages 94–95 in your textbook or visit www.voyagesinenglish.com.

© Loyola Press. Voyages in English Grade 3

4.12 Future Tense with *Going To*

Like *will,* the phrase *going to* is used to express future tense. A form of the helping verb *be* must go in front of *going to.*

Underline the verb in the future tense in each sentence.

1. I am going to paint a picture of my friend.

2. Miriam is going to sing a song.

3. The twins are going to play a game.

4. Gregory is going to clean his room.

5. We are going to sweep the floors.

6. They are going to brush their teeth.

Rewrite each sentence. Change the verb to the future tense with *going to.*

7. We are picking apples in the orchard.

   _____

8. Seth had trimmed the tree.

   _____

9. The mail carrier delivers the mail.

   _____

Write a sentence in the future tense with *going to* for each verb. Use the subject in parentheses.

10. camp (we) _____

11. cook (he) _____

12. rest (I) _____

13. hike (you) _____

14. fish (she) _____

15. swim (they) _____

16. fall (it) _____

© Loyola Press. Voyages in English   Grade 3

For additional help, review pages 96–97 in your textbook
or visit www.voyagesinenglish.com.

Section 4 • 67

4.13 Present Progressive Tense

A verb in the **present progressive tense** tells what is happening now. This tense is formed with *am, is,* or *are* and the present participle.

Underline the verb in the present progressive tense in each sentence.

1. Carmen is sitting by the window.

2. I am solving a word problem.

3. The boys are putting together a puzzle.

4. Wayne is looking for his boots.

5. They are driving to the mountains.

Write a sentence in the present progressive tense for each verb. Use the subject in parentheses.

6. speak (he) _____

7. juggle (they) _____

8. shop (I) _____

9. drip (it) _____

10. explore (we) _____

11. think (she) _____

Rewrite each sentence. Change the verb to the present progressive tense.

12. Someone knocks on the door.

_____

13. Liu rakes the leaves in the front yard.

_____

14. Two runners sprint to the finish line.

_____

15. The turtles sit on the log.

_____

© Loyola Press. Voyages in English   Grade 3

For additional help, review pages 98–99 in your textbook or visit www.voyagesinenglish.com.

4.14 Past Progressive Tense

A verb in the **past progressive tense** tells what was happening in the past. This tense is formed with *was* or *were* and the present participle.

Underline the verb in the past progressive tense in each sentence.

1. We were swimming in the pool.
2. I was resting on the couch after dinner.
3. My friends were waiting at the park.
4. Harry was watering the lawn.
5. The artist was painting a mural on the wall.
6. The manager was closing the store.

Write a sentence in the past progressive tense for each verb. Use the subject in parentheses.

7. listen (she) _____

8. read (I) _____

9. surf (they) _____

10. swing (it) _____

11. relax (we) _____

Rewrite each sentence. Change the verb to the past progressive tense.

12. The red ball bounced down the hill.

_____

13. Several ducks swam across the water.

_____

14. Sierra talked to her friends after school.

_____

15. We searched for Jose's keys.

_____

© Loyola Press. Voyages in English   Grade 3

For additional help, review pages 100–101 in your textbook or visit www.voyagesinenglish.com.

Section 4 • 69

4.15 Is and Are, Was and Were

> *Is, are, was,* and *were* are being verbs. They do not express actions. Use *is* and *was* with singular subjects. Use *are* and *were* with plural subjects.

Circle the verb that correctly completes each sentence.

1. This song (is   are) my favorite.

2. A burrow (is   are) a home for rabbits.

3. The quarterback (was   were) the hero of the game.

4. Those girls (is   are) my older sisters.

5. What (was   were) the answer to the last question?

6. Two students (was   were) late for class today.

7. A chipmunk (is   are) like a squirrel.

8. The customers (was   were) ready for the store to open.

Complete each sentence with *is, are, was,* or *were*. Use the tense shown in parentheses.

9. A haiku _____ one form of poetry. (present)

10. This butterfly _____ once a caterpillar. (past)

11. The Silk Road _____ a famous trade route. (past)

12. These acrobats _____ from China. (present)

13. My tomatoes _____ ready to be picked. (present)

14. The runners _____ tired after the race. (past)

15. This watch _____ a gift from my parents. (past)

16. A flute _____ part of the woodwind section. (present)

Write a sentence for each verb.

17. is _____

18. were _____

19. are _____

© Loyola Press. Voyages in English   Grade 3

For additional help, review pages 102–103 in your textbook or visit www.voyagesinenglish.com.

4.15   *Is and Are, Was and Were*

Is, are, was, and *were* are being verbs. They do not express actions. Use *is* and *was* with singular subjects. Use *are* and *were* with plural subjects.

Complete each sentence with *is, are, was,* or *were*.

1. Jason _____ late for practice yesterday.

2. Mr. Hernandez _____ my new teacher.

3. Those two dogs _____ Labradors.

4. Where _____ you last night?

5. I _____ not ready for that quiz.

6. Much of this state _____ once part of Mexico.

7. Bats _____ mammals.

8. Roald Dahl _____ my favorite author.

Rewrite each sentence correctly. Use *is, are, was,* or *were*.

9. Zebras is herbivores, or plant-eating animals.

   _____

10. Zebras was social animals and live in groups.

    _____

11. A baby zebra were called a foal.

    _____

12. Two kinds of zebras is extinct by the early 20th century.

    _____

13. In Africa in the 1800s, many zebras is hunted.

    _____

14. Today some species of zebras is endangered.

    _____

© Loyola Press. Voyages in English   Grade 3

For additional help, review pages 102–103 in your textbook or visit www.voyagesinenglish.com.

4.16 Contractions with *Not*

A **contraction** is a short way to write some words. An apostrophe (') marks the place where one or more letters have been left out of the words.

Write a contraction for each word or word group.

1. do not _____   **5.** were not _____

2. cannot _____   **6.** does not _____

3. was not _____   **7.** are not _____

4. is not _____   **8.** will not _____

Write a contraction for the underlined word or words in each sentence.

9. Kelly <u>was not</u> ready to leave.   _____

10. They <u>are not</u> staying up late tonight.   _____

11. Tom <u>did not</u> finish his homework.   _____

12. I <u>will not</u> be able to attend the party.   _____

13. Mr. Jameson <u>cannot</u> carry the boxes for you. _____

14. The boys <u>were not</u> running in the hall.   _____

15. We <u>do not</u> have time to clean our rooms.   _____

Rewrite each sentence using a contraction with *not*.

16. We enjoyed the concert in the park.

_____

17. Devin will join the science club.

_____

18. I like tart apples.

_____

19. She can bring the paint for the posters.

_____

© Loyola Press. Voyages in English   Grade 3

For additional help, review pages 104–105 in your textbook or visit www.voyagesinenglish.com.

SECTION 5   **Daily Maintenance**

5.1 **The boy bounces the ball.**

    1. What is the complete subject? _____

    2. What is the complete predicate? _____

    3. Is the verb an action verb or a being verb? _____

    4. Diagram the sentence here.

5.2 **The horses are thirsty.**

    1. Which word is a plural noun? _____

    2. What is the verb? _____

    3. Is the verb an action verb or a being verb? _____

    4. Diagram the sentence here.

5.3 **I might play soccer.**

    1. Is *I* a subject pronoun or an object pronoun? _____

    2. Which word is the main verb? _____

    3. Which word is a helping verb? _____

    4. Diagram the sentence here.

© Loyola Press. Voyages in English   Grade 3

5.4 **Clarissa forgot her homework.**

    1. Is the subject a common or a proper noun?   _____

    2. Which word is a possessive adjective?   _____

    3. Is *forgot* a regular verb or an irregular verb?   _____

    4. Diagram the sentence here.

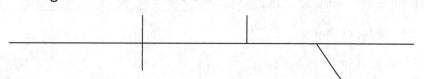

5.5 **He is wearing a blue shirt.**

    1. Is *He* a noun or a pronoun?   _____

    2. Which word is an adjective?   _____

    3. What is the present participle?   _____

    4. Diagram the sentence here.

5.6 **Lynn ate a cheese quesadilla.**

    1. Is the subject simple or compound?   _____

    2. What is the verb?   _____

    3. Is the verb present tense or past tense?   _____

    4. Diagram the sentence here.

© Loyola Press. Voyages in English   **Grade 3**

5.7 **Our class will choose a motto.**

1. Is *Our* a possessive pronoun or adjective? _____

2. What is the verb phrase? _____

3. Is the verb present tense or future tense? _____

4. Diagram the sentence here.

5.8 **The band was playing a song.**

1. Which word is a collective noun? _____

2. What is the verb phrase? _____

3. Is the verb present or past progressive? _____

4. Diagram the sentence here.

5.9 **Dave is rowing the boat.**

1. Which word is a common noun? _____

2. What is the verb phrase? _____

3. Is the verb past or present progressive? _____

4. Diagram the sentence here.

© Loyola Press. Voyages in English   Grade 3

5.10 **The pink bicycle is hers.**

1. What is the simple subject? _____

2. Which word is a possessive pronoun? _____

3. Is the verb an action verb or a being verb? _____

4. Diagram the sentence here.

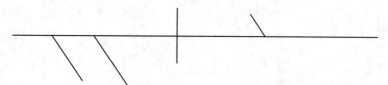

5.11 **Denise wrote a book report.**

1. What is the complete subject? _____

2. Is the verb present tense or past tense? _____

3. Is the verb regular or irregular? _____

4. Diagram the sentence here.

© Loyola Press. Voyages in English **Grade 3**

5.1 Identifying Adjectives

An **adjective** tells more about a noun. Adjectives describe nouns. They can tell how something looks, tastes, sounds, feels, or smells.

Circle the adjective that describes the underlined noun in each sentence.

1. Please help me lift the heavy <u>box</u>.

2. The loud <u>music</u> hurts my ears.

3. Ruby needs a warm <u>blanket</u>.

4. I chose the brown <u>puppy</u>.

5. He put sweet <u>strawberries</u> on the pancakes.

Underline the adjective in each sentence. Circle the noun the adjective describes.

6. The little boy plays on the swings.

7. A noisy rooster woke me up.

8. They ate salty pretzels at the fair.

9. A chinchilla has soft fur.

10. I will wear a blue skirt.

11. He washed the stinky socks.

Add an adjective from the word box to describe each noun. Use the kind of adjective in parentheses.

squeaky	sour	purple	smooth	tall	fragrant

12. the baby's _____ skin (feels)

13. a _____ basketball player (looks)

14. the _____ rose (smells)

15. the _____ apple (tastes)

16. a _____ door (sounds)

17. the _____ grapes (looks)

For additional help, review pages 110–111 in your textbook or visit www.voyagesinenglish.com.

Section 5 • 77

© Loyola Press. Voyages in English   Grade 3

5.2 Adjectives Before Nouns

Most adjectives describe various features of nouns. They are called **descriptive adjectives.** Descriptive adjectives generally come before the nouns they describe.

Underline the descriptive adjectives in each sentence. The number of adjectives is in parentheses.

1. Jeff and I raked the dry leaves. (1)

2. A brown bird sits in a tall tree. (2)

3. The strong wind blew away my new hat. (2)

4. Gray clouds fill the sky. (1)

5. A dark shadow falls across the front yard. (2)

Underline the descriptive adjective in each sentence. Circle the noun the adjective describes.

6. The sun is actually a giant star.

7. It spews hot gas into space.

8. Sunspots are dark areas on the sun.

9. The moon is like a rocky ball.

10. Large craters cover the moon.

11. Some craters could hold a whole city.

Use a descriptive adjective from the word box to complete each sentence. Then underline the noun the adjective describes.

huge	powerful	ancient	magnificent

12. The _____ Egyptians built pyramids.

13. Each pyramid was made of _____ stone blocks.

14. The pyramids were _____ tombs for the pharaohs.

15. Pharaohs were the _____ rulers of Egypt.

© Loyola Press. Voyages in English   Grade 3

For additional help, review pages 112–113 in your textbook or visit www.voyagesinenglish.com.

5.3 Subject Complements

Some descriptive adjectives come after a being verb. They are called **subject complements.** An adjective used as a subject complement tells more about the subject of the sentence.

Underline the adjective used as a subject complement in each sentence.

1. A day at the carnival is exciting.

2. The roller-coaster ride was scary.

3. The line for the sky ride is long.

4. These games are fun.

5. This bottle of water is cold.

6. After a long day, my feet were sore.

Underline the adjective used as a subject complement in each sentence. Circle the noun the subject complement describes.

7. The kitten's fur is soft.

8. Our trip to the zoo was informative.

9. The rabbits in this cage are large.

10. That movie was hilarious.

11. The boy's boots are muddy.

12. This math test is difficult.

Use each word as the subject complement in a sentence. Then underline the noun the subject complement describes.

13. small _____

14. beautiful _____

15. hot _____

16. sharp _____

17. loud _____

18. tasty _____

© Loyola Press. Voyages in English   Grade 3

For additional help, review pages 114–115 in your textbook or visit www.voyagesinenglish.com.

Section 5 • 79

5.4   Compound Subject Complements

Two adjectives joined by *and* or *or* after a being verb form a **compound subject complement.** Both adjectives tell more about the subject.

Circle the adjectives used as subject complements in each sentence. Then circle *yes* or *no* to tell whether the subject complement is compound.

1. The berries we picked are red and sweet.   yes   no

2. Dan's story is very good.   yes   no

3. The candles on the table are tall and bright.   yes   no

4. The baseball game was long.   yes   no

5. Those jellyfish are colorful.   yes   no

6. We can buy roses that are yellow or pink.   yes   no

7. The city bus was slow and late.   yes   no

8. That Greek salad was delicious.   yes   no

9. Roger's watch is old and valuable.   yes   no

Complete each sentence with a compound subject complement.

10. The racehorses are _____ and _____.

11. The elephants are _____ and _____.

12. Those giraffes are _____ and _____.

13. My hamster is _____ and _____.

14. John's snakes are _____ and _____.

Use each adjective pair to write a sentence with a compound subject complement.

15. hot and thirsty _____

_____

16. clean and neat _____

_____

© Loyola Press. Voyages in English   Grade 3

For additional help, review pages 116–117 in your textbook or visit www.voyagesinenglish.com.

5.5 Adjectives That Compare

Adjectives can be used to make comparisons. To compare two or more nouns, *-er* is often added to an adjective. To compare three or more nouns, *-est* is usually added to the adjective.

Complete the chart.

ADJECTIVE	COMPARE TWO NOUNS	COMPARE THREE OR MORE NOUNS
1. big	_____	_____
2. high	_____	_____
3. deep	_____	_____
4. heavy	_____	_____
5. close	_____	_____
6. sunny	_____	_____
7. noisy	_____	_____

Underline the adjective that compares in each sentence.

8. My dog is smaller than Alice's dog.

9. Demarcus is the tallest player on the team.

10. This is the quickest route home.

11. Her pillow is the softest of the four on the sofa.

12. This cartoon was funnier than that one.

13. Luka's room is neater than mine.

Circle the adjective that correctly completes each sentence.

14. Larry's pumpkin is the (smaller   smallest) of all.

15. A boa constrictor is (longer   longest) than a rattlesnake.

16. My sister is (older   oldest) than my brother.

17. Use the (larger   largest) pot you have.

18. Becky made the (tastier   tastiest) dish in the cooking contest.

For additional help, review pages 118–119 in your textbook or visit www.voyagesinenglish.com.

Section 5 • 81

© Loyola Press. Voyages in English   Grade 3

5.6 Irregular Adjectives That Compare

Some adjectives that compare are irregular. They are not formed by adding *-er* or *-est*. Two common irregular adjectives are *good* and *bad*.

Circle the correct adjective to complete each sentence.

1. Vanessa is a (good   better) dancer than Mimi.

2. That was the (worse   worst) movie I've ever seen.

3. A (good   best) form of exercise is yoga.

4. Sugar is (bad   worse) for your teeth.

5. Grandma makes the (best   good) blueberry muffins.

6. The rain today is (worse   worst) than yesterday.

7. I am a (better   best) singer than Judy.

Write *good, better,* or *best* to complete each sentence.

8. Jen is the _____ singer in the choir.

9. A _____ outdoor activity is walking.

10. The children had a _____ time at the park.

11. Your suggestion is _____ than mine.

12. Tanya is a _____ tennis player than Colleen.

13. Lionel is my _____ friend.

Write *bad, worse,* or *worst* to complete each sentence.

14. My fever is _____ today than yesterday.

15. What is the _____ book you have read?

16. That was our _____ game this season.

17. I got a _____ grade on my report.

18. The child was punished for his _____ behavior.

19. His performance was _____ than yours.

© Loyola Press. Voyages in English   Grade 3

For additional help, review pages 120–121 in your textbook or visit www.voyagesinenglish.com.

5.7 Adjectives That Tell How Many

Adjectives can tell how many or about how many. Adjectives that tell how many include numbers, such as *one* or *twenty*. These adjectives also include words that tell numerical order, such as *first* or *second*.

Underline the adjective. Write whether the adjective tells *about* how many or *exactly* how many.

1. many people _____

2. six servers _____

3. one elevator _____

4. second floor _____

5. some signs _____

6. several customers _____

Underline the adjective that tells how many in each sentence. Write whether the adjective tells *about how many* or *exactly how many*.

7. There are many cars in the parking lot. _____

8. You need three cups of flour. _____

9. I'll take a dozen bagels. _____

10. A few birds are sitting in the tree. _____

11. Several students are absent today. _____

12. I sit in the fifth row. _____

Complete each sentence with an adjective that tells how many. Use the directions in parentheses.

13. There are _____ players on our team. (exactly how many)

14. I read _____ books over the summer. (about how many)

15. _____ children played in the sand. (about how many)

16. We need _____ tomatoes for the soup. (exactly how many)

17. _____ people are walking in the rain. (about how many)

© Loyola Press. Voyages in English   Grade 3

For additional help, review pages 122–123 in your textbook or visit www.voyagesinenglish.com.

Section 5 • 83

5.8 Articles

The, *an*, and *a* point out nouns. They are called **articles.** Use *a* before a word that begins with a consonant sound. Use *an* before a word that begins with a vowel sound.

Underline the articles in each sentence.

1. The animals sleep in the barn.

2. The animals drink from a trough.

3. A farmer drives a tractor.

4. A foal is a baby horse.

5. An orchard is a field of fruit trees.

6. The horse eats an apple.

Add *a* or *an* before each noun.

7. _____ forest   12. _____ planet

8. _____ umbrella   13. _____ orange

9. _____ airport   14. _____ letter

10. _____ engine   15. _____ icicle

11. _____ window   16. _____ photo

Choose the correct articles to complete the sentences.

17. We saw (a   an) elephant at (the   an) zoo.

18. Gina works at (a   an) clothing store.

19. I have (a   an) idea for (the   an) talent show.

20. (An   The) dog is digging (a   an) hole.

21. (A   An) grater is (a   an) kitchen tool.

22. (An   The) girl is holding (a   an) balloon.

23. (A   An) earthquake shook (the   an) city.

24. (A   An) orchestra is (a   an) group of musicians.

© Loyola Press. Voyages in English   Grade 3

For additional help, review pages 124–125 in your textbook or visit www.voyagesinenglish.com.

5.9 Demonstrative Adjectives

Demonstrative adjectives point out or tell about a specific person, place, or thing. *This* and *these* point out something that is near. *That* and *those* point out something that is farther away.

Write *this* or *these* to show that the things are near.

1. _____ blanket   4. _____ pillow

2. _____ towels   5. _____ bed

3. _____ sheets   6. _____ socks

Write *that* or *those* to show that the things are far away.

7. _____ pots   10. _____ spoon

8. _____ pans   11. _____ timer

9. _____ tray   12. _____ plates

Underline the demonstrative adjective in each sentence. Write whether the adjective tells about something that is *near* or *far away*.

13. These mice are sleeping.   _____

14. I like that kitten.   _____

15. Those parakeets are noisy.   _____

16. We will buy this aquarium.   _____

17. Did you see that baby guinea pig?   _____

18. This red collar is for Princess.   _____

19. Duke is playing with those dog toys.   _____

Write a sentence that includes a demonstrative adjective before each subject.

20. a plane that is far away

_____

21. chairs that are near

_____

© Loyola Press. Voyages in English   Grade 3

For additional help, review pages 126–127 in your textbook or visit www.voyagesinenglish.com.

Section 5 • 85

5.10 Proper Adjectives

A proper noun names a particular person, place, or thing. Some adjectives are formed from proper nouns. These adjectives are called **proper adjectives.**

Circle the proper adjective in each pair of words.

1. Canada   Canadian
2. Mexican   Mexico
3. Chinese   China

4. India   Indian
5. Egypt   Egyptian
6. Italian   Italy

Underline the proper adjective in each sentence. Circle the noun the adjective describes.

7. We ate Greek food for dinner.

8. Hawaiian orchids are beautiful.

9. Richard showed me some Spanish coins.

10. Jamaican music is my favorite.

11. This Texan chili is very spicy.

12. A kimono is a Japanese garment.

13. The Irish dancers performed for us.

14. The Brazilian beaches were very crowded.

Complete each sentence with the proper adjective for the proper noun in parentheses. Use a dictionary if you need help.

15. The Fourth of July is an _____ holiday. (America)

16. I am learning about _____ culture. (Korea)

17. We bought _____ sausage at the store. (Poland)

18. The _____ gymnasts won the contest. (Romania)

19. This restaurant serves _____ food. (France)

20. We traveled through the _____ outback. (Australia)

21. Which _____ countries can you name? (Africa)

© Loyola Press. Voyages in English   Grade 3

For additional help, review pages 128–129 in your textbook or visit www.voyagesinenglish.com.

5.11 Nouns Used as Adjectives

Sometimes a noun can be used as an adjective. When two nouns are used together, the first noun often acts as an adjective. It tells about the second noun.

Write whether the underlined word is used as a *noun* or as an *adjective*.

1. I am on a <u>baseball</u> team.   _____

2. Throw me the <u>baseball</u>.   _____

3. I drank <u>orange</u> juice with my breakfast.   _____

4. This <u>orange</u> tastes sweet.   _____

5. We swam in the <u>ocean</u>.   _____

6. Our room has an <u>ocean</u> view.   _____

Underline all the nouns in each sentence. Write the noun used as an adjective.

7. The dinosaur exhibit was fascinating.   _____

8. My aunt lives in an apartment building.   _____

9. His father is our soccer coach.   _____

10. The police officers patrol the streets.   _____

11. My beach towel has a picture of a fish on it. _____

12. An ambulance is an emergency vehicle.   _____

Write two sentences for each word. Use it once as a noun and once as an adjective. Write how you used the word in each sentence.

13. winter _____

    _____

14. storm _____

    _____

15. school _____

    _____

For additional help, review pages 130–131 in your textbook or visit www.voyagesinenglish.com.

Section 5 • 87

© Loyola Press. Voyages in English Grade 3

SECTION 6 **Daily Maintenance**

6.1 **The tall giraffe is eating green leaves.**

1. What is the verb phrase?   _____

2. What is the plural noun?   _____

3. Which words are adjectives?   _____

4. Diagram the sentence here.

6.2 **The red apple tastes sweet.**

1. What is the simple subject?   _____

2. What is the simple predicate?   _____

3. Which adjective is a subject complement?   _____

4. Diagram the sentence here.

6.3 **The best dish was the lasagna.**

1. Is *dish* a singular noun or a plural noun? _____

2. Is the verb an action verb or a being verb? _____

3. Which word is an irregular adjective?   _____

4. Diagram the sentence here.

© Loyola Press. Voyages in English **Grade 3**

6.4 **The reporter interviewed several people.**

1. Which word is a plural noun? _____

2. Is the verb regular or irregular? _____

3. Which adjective tells about how many? _____

4. Diagram the sentence here.

6.5 **My sister caught the biggest fish.**

1. What is the complete subject? _____

2. What is the complete predicate? _____

3. Which word is a superlative adjective? _____

4. Diagram the sentence here.

6.6 **The cleaner room is mine.**

1. Is the subject singular or plural? _____

2. Is *mine* a pronoun or an adjective? _____

3. Which word is a comparative adjective? _____

4. Diagram the sentence here.

© Loyola Press. Voyages in English   Grade 3

6.7 **The hungry bird caught a worm.**

    1. What is the simple subject?   _____

    2. Is the verb regular or irregular?   _____

    3. Which words are articles?   _____

    4. Diagram the sentence here.

6.8 **She might buy this coat.**

    1. Is the subject a noun or a pronoun?   _____

    2. Which word is a helping verb?   _____

    3. Which word is a demonstrative adjective? _____

    4. Diagram the sentence here.

6.9 **I will make the French toast.**

    1. What is the verb phrase?   _____

    2. Is the tense simple past or simple future? _____

    3. Which word is a proper adjective?   _____

    4. Diagram the sentence here.

© Loyola Press. Voyages in English **Grade 3**

6.1   Adverbs

An **adverb** tells more about a verb. Some adverbs tell when, where, or how something happens. Many adverbs end in *ly*.

Underline the adverb in each sentence.

1. Let's walk slowly through the garden.
2. Today I'm going to finish this book.
3. Juan put the cat inside for the night.
4. Handle the eggs carefully.
5. Ramona went outside to get the mail.
6. Allan always takes a lunch to school.
7. The students walked calmly to the exit.
8. Those children are playing upstairs.

Write an adverb from the word box to complete each sentence.

nervously	often	yesterday	tomorrow	slowly	there

9. The shy girl _____ stood before the class.
10. We went to the aquarium _____.
11. The old dog walked _____ down the street.
12. _____ we will drive to the lake.
13. You can set up the tent _____.
14. My best friend lives nearby, so we _____ play together.

Write an adverb to complete each sentence. Have the adverb tell what is in parentheses.

15. Sandra _____ finished her homework. (how)
16. The music store at the mall is located _____. (where)
17. I _____ miss soccer practice. (when)
18. The movie will begin _____. (when)

© Loyola Press. Voyages in English   Grade 3

For additional help, review pages 136–137 in your textbook or visit www.voyagesinenglish.com.

6.2 Adverbs That Tell When or How Often

An adverb tells more about a verb. Some adverbs tell when or how often something happens.

Underline the adverb that tells when or how often in each sentence.

1. Adam hurt his ankle again.

2. The girls arrived at the dance early.

3. I sometimes ride my bike to Meg's house.

4. Then the bird flew to its nest.

5. The newspaper arrives at their home daily.

6. We frequently see deer in our backyard.

7. Shane is going to the dentist today.

8. Colleen never forgets to do her chores.

Circle the adverb that correctly completes each sentence.

9. We are going camping (yesterday   tomorrow).

10. (First   Never), I pack our camping gear.

11. (Then   Weekly) Mike fills an ice chest with food.

12. (Forever   Now) we drive to the campground.

13. We will set up the tent (often   later).

14. Everyone will gaze at the stars (daily   tonight).

Write adverbs that tell when or how often to complete the sentences.

15. I _____ eat _____.

16. My friends and I _____ play _____.

17. At school I read books _____.

18. On the weekend my family _____ goes to the library.

19. During the summer my family and I _____ remain

_____.

© Loyola Press. Voyages in English   Grade 3

For additional help, review pages 138–139 in your textbook or visit www.voyagesinenglish.com.

6.3 | Adverbs That Tell Where

Some adverbs tell where something takes place. These adverbs answer the question *where*.

Underline the adverb that tells where in each sentence.

1. Dad moved the chairs inside.

2. The boat moved forward in the water.

3. Who let the dogs in?

4. Pablo came downstairs to eat dinner.

5. Mai is going away for the weekend.

6. We watched the ducks swim nearby.

7. I have looked everywhere for my gym bag.

8. Please leave your muddy boots outside.

Write an adverb from the word box to complete each sentence.

downstairs	nearby	backward	inside	above	up

9. A flock of parrots flies _____.

10. We rushed _____ to escape the rain.

11. The protective cat keeps her kittens _____.

12. Walk _____ to get to the ground floor.

13. I stepped _____ when I saw the snake.

14. They rode the ski lift _____.

Write an adverb that tells where to complete each sentence.

15. I go to the park _____.

16. I meet my friends _____.

17. It feels good to play _____.

18. At the big hill, we tumble _____.

© Loyola Press. Voyages in English   Grade 3

For additional help, review pages 140–141 in your textbook or visit www.voyagesinenglish.com.

6.4 Adverbs That Tell How

Some adverbs tell how an action takes place. These adverbs answer the question *how*.

Underline the adverb that tells how in each sentence.

1. Patty carefully read her report.

2. Mike slowly ate his dinner.

3. Both students walked proudly home.

4. I will hold the baby gently.

5. The elephant stomped noisily through the jungle.

6. We must talk quietly about the surprise party.

7. He waited sadly by the steps.

8. The player swung clumsily at the ball.

Write an adverb from the word box to complete each sentence.

quietly	loudly	gingerly	hard	quickly	safely

9. The crossing guard helps us _____ cross the street.

10. The batter hit the ball _____ and scored the winning run.

11. Robby walked _____ on his sprained ankle.

12. Students in the library must talk _____.

13. This horse ran _____ and won the race.

14. The car alarm rang _____.

Rewrite each sentence with an adverb that tells how.

15. Your brother dances.

_____

16. These students work.

_____

© Loyola Press. Voyages in English   Grade 3

For additional help, review pages 142–143 in your textbook or visit www.voyagesinenglish.com.

6.5 Negative Words

A negative idea is formed by adding *not* to the verb, by adding *not* as part of a contraction, or by adding *never* before the verb. Because these negative words tell about verbs, they are adverbs.

Underline the negative word in each sentence.

1. My sister never cleans her room.

2. You should not waste paper.

3. We can't find the basketball.

4. Jacob didn't like the movie.

5. She will not attend the meeting.

6. Our dog never misses a meal.

Rewrite each sentence so that it correctly expresses a negative idea.

7. We don't never miss the school bus.

   _____

8. Rashad won't have no trouble scoring a goal.

   _____

9. She didn't find no dress at the mall.

   _____

Rewrite each sentence so that it expresses a negative idea.

10. The dog barks.

   _____

11. I am afraid of spiders.

   _____

12. Charlotte is a good singer.

   _____

© Loyola Press. Voyages in English   Grade 3

For additional help, review pages 144–145 in your textbook or visit www.voyagesinenglish.com.

6.6 Good and Well

> *Good* is an adjective that describes a noun. It tells what kind. *Well* is an adverb that tells about a verb. It tells how.

Add *good* or *well* to each group of words.

1. can paint _____

2. storyteller _____

3. suggestion _____

4. does cook _____

5. serves the ball _____

6. restaurant _____

Write *good* or *well* to complete each sentence.

7. Ray is a _____ tennis player.

8. He plays the game _____.

9. My friend Nancy speaks _____.

10. She gave a _____ oral report.

11. My father is a _____ cook.

12. He prepares _____ meals for us.

13. Mischa does not roller-skate _____.

14. However, she skis very _____.

Write a sentence for each word. Use *good* or *well* in the sentence.

15. dance _____

16. artist _____

17. coach _____

18. writes _____

19. sing _____

20. story _____

© Loyola Press. Voyages in English   Grade 3

For additional help, review pages 146–147 in your textbook or visit www.voyagesinenglish.com.

6.7   *To, Too,* and *Two*

To, too, and *two* sound alike, but each word has a different meaning. *To* means "in the direction of" or "until." *Too* means "also" or "more than enough." *Two* means "the number 2."

Circle the word that correctly completes each sentence.

1. I sent a letter (to   too) my pen pal.

2. It is (to   too) cold to play outside.

3. That road leads (to   two) their farm.

4. Wayne went to the movie (two   too).

5. This toy costs (two   too) dollars.

6. The play will begin in (two   to) minutes.

Write *to, too,* or *two* to complete each sentence.

7. I have _____ pets.

8. This movie lasts _____ hours.

9. They are walking _____ the park.

10. The carnival runs from Friday _____ Sunday.

11. Victor is in this class _____.

12. This large box is _____ heavy.

13. Can you go _____ the science center with us?

Rewrite each sentence correctly.

14. Heather plays softball to.

_____

15. I won too stuffed animals.

_____

16. Elena wants too go too.

_____

For additional help, review pages 148–149 in your textbook
or visit www.voyagesinenglish.com.

Section 6 • 97

© Loyola Press. Voyages in English   Grade 3

6.8 *Their* and *There*

> *Their* and *there* sound alike but have different meanings. *Their* is an adjective and tells who owns something. *There* is an adverb and usually means "in that place."

Write *yes* or *no* to identify whether *their* or *there* are used correctly in each sentence.

1. Their uniforms are blue and white. _____

2. It is too expensive to eat their. _____

3. They wash there hands before meals. _____

4. Let's sit there for our picnic. _____

5. We visited them at their new home. _____

6. You can put your coat over their. _____

Circle the word that correctly completes each sentence.

7. The girls' restroom is (their   there).

8. Place your library books (their   there).

9. Have you seen (their   there) new dog?

10. Wait (their   there) for the next clerk.

11. The students take out (their   there) books.

12. These are (their   there) class pictures.

13. Have you eaten (their   there) before?

Write *their* or *there* to complete each sentence.

14. Put the costumes _____.

15. Bob and Lucy are trying on _____ costumes.

16. The actors rehearse _____ lines for the play.

17. You can paint the scenery _____.

18. Stand _____ for the first scene.

19. The audience excitedly claps _____ hands.

© Loyola Press. Voyages in English **Grade 3**

For additional help, review pages 150–151 in your textbook or visit www.voyagesinenglish.com.

6.9   Coordinating Conjunctions

A **coordinating conjunction** joins two words or groups of words. The words *and, but,* and *or* are coordinating conjunctions.

Underline the coordinating conjunction in each sentence.

1. Kwan eats corn but not broccoli.

2. You can make the tacos or grate the cheese.

3. I bought shoes and a shirt.

4. Their home is small but cozy.

5. The dog has small ears and a short tail.

6. Christine will play volleyball or basketball.

Circle the coordinating conjunction in each sentence. Underline the words or groups of words that the conjunction joins.

7. We can order soup or salad.

8. John is noisy but shy.

9. The kittens are sleeping on the bed and in the basket.

10. This green salsa is spicy but tasty.

11. Taylor does not like to cook or clean.

12. We walked over the bridge and along the stream.

Write *and, but,* or *or* to complete each sentence.

13. The children are catching butterflies _____ ladybugs.

14. At the beach we can sail _____ surf.

15. I added tomato _____ cucumber to the salad.

16. The tour was long _____ informative.

17. She will sit on the beach _____ by the pool.

18. These trees' trunks are thin _____ strong.

19. Johnny wants to be a firefighter _____ a police officer.

© Loyola Press. Voyages in English   Grade 3

For additional help, review pages 152–153 in your textbook or visit www.voyagesinenglish.com.

6.9 Coordinating Conjunctions

A **coordinating conjunction** joins two words or groups of words. The words *and, but,* and *or* are coordinating conjunctions.

Circle the coordinating conjunction in each sentence. Underline the words or groups of words that the conjunction joins.

1. Deer and rabbits come out at dusk.

2. Miriam will buy and wrap the gifts.

3. This equipment is expensive but necessary.

4. These cows are large but gentle.

5. Some animals are kept in barns or pens.

6. We can sit on the deck or under the tree.

7. The fans clapped their hands and stomped their feet.

Rewrite each sentence using the correct coordinating conjunction.

8. The package should arrive on Monday and Tuesday.

_____

9. Our dog is small or strong.

_____

10. He mowed the lawn or trimmed the trees.

_____

11. The blender is on the counter but in the cupboard.

_____

Write a sentence for each coordinating conjunction. Then underline the words or groups of words the coordinating conjunction joins.

12. and _____

13. but _____

14. or _____

© Loyola Press. Voyages in English   Grade 3

For additional help, review pages 152–153 in your textbook or visit www.voyagesinenglish.com.

SECTION 7 | Daily Maintenance

7.1 **The children quickly finished their chores.**

1. What is the complete subject?   _____

2. What is the simple predicate?   _____

3. Which word is an adverb?   _____

4. Diagram the sentence here.

7.2 **Today we are planting a garden.**

1. What is the helping verb?   _____

2. Is the pronoun singular or plural?   _____

3. Which word is an adverb?   _____

4. Diagram the sentence here.

7.3 **Rosa often tells funny stories.**

1. Which word is a plural noun?   _____

2. Is *funny* used as an adjective or an adverb? _____

3. Which word is an adverb?   _____

4. Diagram the sentence here.

© Loyola Press. Voyages in English   Grade 3

7.4 **Jim and Jason are playing outside.**

1. Is the subject simple or compound? _____

2. Which word is a present participle? _____

3. Which word is an adverb? _____

4. Diagram the sentence here.

7.5 **My sister holds the baby gently.**

1. Is the verb regular or irregular? _____

2. Which words are nouns? _____

3. Which word is an adverb? _____

4. Diagram the sentence here.

7.6 **Chris never forgets his homework.**

1. What tense is the verb? _____

2. Is *his* an adjective or a pronoun? _____

3. Which word is an adverb? _____

4. Diagram the sentence here.

© Loyola Press. Voyages in English Grade 3

7.7 **The new coach is good.**

1. What is the simple subject? _____

2. Which word is a subject complement? _____

3. Is *good* an adjective or an adverb? _____

4. Diagram the sentence here.

7.8 **Lindsey can play the violin well.**

1. What is the complete subject? _____

2. Which word is a direct object? _____

3. Is *well* an adjective or an adverb? _____

4. Diagram the sentence here.

7.9 **Mrs. Tanaka will display the paintings there.**

1. Which word is an article? _____

2. What tense is the verb phrase? _____

3. Which word is an adverb? _____

4. Diagram the sentence here.

© Loyola Press. Voyages in English **Grade 3**

7.10 **I left mine upstairs.**

1. Is the subject pronoun singular or plural?   _____

2. Is *mine* an adjective or a pronoun?   _____

3. Which word is an adverb?   _____

4. Diagram the sentence here.

7.11 **Cats and dogs are good pets.**

1. Which words are nouns?   _____

2. What is the linking verb?   _____

3. Which word is a coordinating conjunction?   _____

4. Diagram the sentence here.

© Loyola Press. Voyages in English   Grade 3

7.1 End Punctuation

A sentence that tells something ends with a **period.** A sentence that asks a question ends with a **question mark.** A sentence that expresses strong or sudden feeling ends with an **exclamation point.**

Circle whether each sentence tells something (*TS*), asks a question (*AQ*), or expresses a strong feeling (*EF*).

1. How was your summer vacation?   TS   AQ   EF
2. We went to the beach.   TS   AQ   EF
3. Kelly went camping in the mountains.   TS   AQ   EF
4. How exciting that is!   TS   AQ   EF
5. Were you cold?   TS   AQ   EF
6. It can be chilly in the mountains.   TS   AQ   EF
7. What a long hike we took!   TS   AQ   EF
8. We hiked 10 miles in one day.   TS   AQ   EF

Add the correct punctuation at the end of each sentence.

9. This is my dog
10. What a huge animal that is
11. What is your dog's name
12. His name is Patches
13. Can he do any tricks
14. Yes, he can shake hands
15. I wish I had a dog

Write three sentences about a favorite place. Use a different punctuation mark at the end of each sentence.

16. _____

17. _____

18. _____

© Loyola Press. Voyages in English   Grade 3

For additional help, review pages 158–159 in your textbook or visit www.voyagesinenglish.com.

7.2 Capitalization

Certain words always begin with a capital letter. The exact name of a person, place, or thing begins with a capital letter. The personal pronoun *I* is always a capital letter.

Circle why each word or word group uses a capital letter.

1. January   name of a day   name of a month
2. Sharon   name of a street   name of a person
3. Valentine's Day   name of a holiday   name of a state
4. our cat, Fluffy   name of a pet   name of a person
5. Australia   name of a city   name of a country
6. Oak Avenue   name of a street   name of a city
7. Montana   name of a holiday   name of a state
8. Dallas   name of a city   name of a month

Underline the letters in each sentence that should be capital letters.

9. my sister's favorite holiday is thanksgiving.

10. this is our cousin sonya from england.

11. our school will be closed on monday.

12. karina and i were both born in may.

13. melissa lives on foothill street.

14. jonah moved to toledo, ohio.

15. i think cesar chavez was a hero.

Write sentences using the name of a city, a street, and a person. Use capital letters correctly.

16. _____

17. _____

18. _____

© Loyola Press. Voyages in English   Grade 3

For additional help, review pages 160–161 in your textbook or visit www.voyagesinenglish.com.

7.3 Abbreviations

An **abbreviation** is a short form of a word. Abbreviations often end
with periods. Abbreviations for units of measure do not begin with
capital letters.

Rewrite each word group, using the abbreviation for each underlined word.

1. South Orange Street   _____

2. one inch of ribbon   _____

3. Pine Avenue   _____

4. one pint of sour cream   _____

5. Friday, April 5   _____

6. North Lincoln Boulevard   _____

7. Monday, September 20   _____

8. one quart of apple juice _____

9. Sunday, February 10   _____

Write the word for each abbreviation.

10. Sat. _____   14. Rd. _____

11. ft. _____   15. yd. _____

12. E. _____   16. Thurs. _____

13. Aug. _____   17. Dec. _____

Rewrite each sentence, using abbreviations correctly.

18. The package should arrive on Tue. or Weds.

_____

19. Our vacation lasts from Jun. to aug.

_____

20. This recipe requires one Qt of milk.

_____

© Loyola Press. Voyages in English   Grade 3

For additional help, review pages 162–163 in your textbook
or visit www.voyagesinenglish.com.

7.4 Personal Titles and Initials

The titles *Mr., Mrs., Ms., Dr., Gov.,* and *Capt.* are abbreviations. Each one begins with a capital letter and ends with a period. A person might use an initial. An initial is a capital letter followed by a period.

Rewrite these names, using periods and capital letters.

1. mrs aretha p williams   _____

2. mr enrique m morales   _____

3. c j parker   _____

4. dr john d ellison   _____

5. gov damien franklin   _____

6. capt allison mayes   _____

Rewrite each sentence. Use periods and capital letters where they are needed. Use abbreviations where you can.

7. mrs savannah c harkins works in the school office

_____

8. The person in charge is captain aaron m sanders

_____

9. mayor choi honored mr a j smith for his community service

_____

10. doctor ashvin patel is my pediatrician

_____

11. The last speaker will be governor alexis bradshaw

_____

12. i sent an invitation to ms gabriela gomez

_____

© Loyola Press. Voyages in English   Grade 3

For additional help, review pages 164–165 in your textbook or visit www.voyagesinenglish.com.

7.5 Titles of Books and Poems

There are special rules for writing the **titles of books and poems.** Each important word in a title begins with a capital letter. Underline the title of a book. Put quotation marks around the title of a poem.

Write whether each title is a *book* or a *poem*.

1. <u>James and the Giant Peach</u> by Roald Dahl _____

2. "An Elephant Is Hard to Hide" by Jack Prelutsky _____

3. <u>Runaway Ralph</u> by Beverly Cleary _____

4. <u>The Best School Year Ever</u> by Barbara Robinson _____

5. "Tree House" by Shel Silverstein _____

6. "Every Time I Climb a Tree" by David McCord _____

7. <u>Anansi the Spider</u> by Gerald McDermott _____

Write each title correctly. Use quotation marks, underlining, and capital letters where they are needed.

8. charlotte's web (book)

_____

9. if i were ruler of the world (poem)

_____

10. getting dressed for school (poem)

_____

11. the boxcar children (book)

_____

12. when i was young in the mountains (book)

_____

13. the midnight ride of paul revere (poem)

_____

© Loyola Press. Voyages in English   Grade 3

For additional help, review pages 166–167 in your textbook or visit www.voyagesinenglish.com.

7.6   Commas in a Series

Three or more words or groups of words of the same kind written one after another are called a **series.** Commas are used to separate words in a series so they are easier to read.

Add commas to separate the words in a series.

1. tulips daisies and sunflowers

2. potatoes tomatoes and carrots

3. shovel rake and gloves

4. water sunlight and air

5. digging planting and watering

6. stem roots and petals

7. Saturday Sunday and Monday

Rewrite each sentence. Add commas to separate the words in a series.

8. We picked apples peaches and plums.

    _____

9. I saw deer squirrels and raccoons.

    _____

10. Pink purple and red are Sheila's favorite colors.

    _____

11. They will buy bread cheese and salami.

    _____

12. Spain Italy and France are the countries we visited.

    _____

13. We can swim sail or hike at camp.

    _____

© Loyola Press. Voyages in English Grade 3

For additional help, review pages 168–169 in your textbook or visit www.voyagesinenglish.com.

7.7 Commas in Direct Address

Speaking directly to a person and using that person's name is called **direct address.** Commas are used to set off the name of the person spoken to from the rest of the sentence.

Underline the name in direct address in each sentence. Then add a comma or commas where they are needed.

1. Becky please help me carry this box.

2. I hope Tom that you have the key.

3. Ms. Hamilton has the bell rung yet?

4. Be careful with those scissors Ruben.

5. Crystal I don't know the answer.

6. To make the team Deshawn you must practice every day.

7. We found your backpack Grace.

8. This painting Rob is the one I bought.

9. Joanna put the clothes in the dryer.

Rewrite each sentence, using commas correctly.

10. Suzy go to the store, to buy some milk.

    _____

11. Please pass, me, the potatoes Avery.

    _____

12. Oh, Mia you've spilled the paint!

    _____

13. Help, me, Juan clean out the garage.

    _____

14. Do, you, need a ride home Lara?

    _____

For additional help, review pages 170–171 in your textbook or visit www.voyagesinenglish.com.

Section 7 • 111

© Loyola Press. Voyages in English   Grade 3

7.8 Commas in Compound Sentences

A comma is used when two short sentences are combined into a **compound sentence.** To make a compound sentence, use a comma followed by *and, but*, or *or* to join two sentences.

Add a comma where it is needed in each sentence.

1. Kevin wanted the job but he did not get it.

2. Misty might walk to school or she might ride her bike.

3. I peeled the potatoes and Ally chopped them into pieces.

4. Rain poured down and everyone rushed inside.

5. It is time to slice the turkey but Dad can't find the knife.

6. Arthur will read a book or he will take a nap.

7. Michelle and I started our homework and we finished in an hour.

Rewrite each pair of sentences as a compound sentence. Add a comma and the word *and* or *but* to join the sentences.

8. My sister enjoys singing. I prefer dancing.

   _____

9. I ran to the corner. The bus had already left.

   _____

10. Mr. Ramos teaches math. He coaches the soccer team.

    _____

11. The cars raced around the track. They headed for the finish line.

    _____

12. The squirrel ran away. It climbed up the tree.

    _____

13. Jane brought her baseball glove. She forgot her bat.

    _____

© Loyola Press. Voyages in English Grade 3

For additional help, review pages 172–173 in your textbook or visit www.voyagesinenglish.com.

7.8 Commas in Compound Sentences

> A comma is used when two short sentences are combined into a **compound sentence.** To make a compound sentence, use a comma followed by *and, but*, or *or* to join two sentences.

Rewrite each pair of sentences as a compound sentence.

1. Lily tried on the dress. She didn't buy it.

   _____

2. The boys can play a game. They can watch a DVD.

   _____

3. Emily washed the dishes. I dried them.

   _____

4. We went fishing. We didn't catch anything.

   _____

Add commas where they are needed for a series, a name in direct address, or a compound sentence.

5. Paolo where is your report?

6. The recipe needs potatoes carrots and corn.

7. I called Steve but he wasn't home.

8. We can ski sled or skate.

9. Trish plays the flute and Mitch plays the clarinet.

10. Please take out the trash Dennis.

11. The players might practice drills or they might run laps.

Complete each short sentence. Then combine them into a compound sentence.

12. I like to _____. My friend likes to _____.

    _____

For additional help, review pages 172–173 in your textbook or visit www.voyagesinenglish.com.

Section 7 • 113

© Loyola Press. Voyages in English   Grade 3

7.9 Apostrophes

The **apostrophe** is a punctuation mark used in several ways. An apostrophe is used to form the possessive of a noun or to replace letters left out in a contraction.

Write whether the apostrophe in each sentence shows *possession* or forms a *contraction*.

1. I like Ana's new haircut. _____

2. We don't have any more bread. _____

3. The money isn't in my wallet. _____

4. Brandy's house is close to mine. _____

5. This is Mario's desk. _____

6. My parents can't attend the play tonight. _____

7. The dogs aren't in the backyard. _____

8. Amir's sister walked him to school. _____

Add an apostrophe where it is needed in each sentence.

9. Hailey doesnt like spinach.

10. We enjoyed Clarks exciting story.

11. Hopes aquarium is very large.

12. Jeff wont forget his homework again.

13. You shouldnt leave the window open.

14. Stella is wrapping Carls gift.

15. Have you met Raquels parents?

16. I wasnt ready for the test.

Write two sentences. Include a possessive noun in one sentence and a contraction in the other sentence. Use apostrophes correctly.

17. _____

18. _____

© Loyola Press. Voyages in English Grade 3

For additional help, review pages 174–175 in your textbook or visit www.voyagesinenglish.com.

7.10 Addresses

In an **address,** the first letter of every word and abbreviation is capitalized. A comma separates the street address and the apartment or floor number and also the city and the state.

Underline the letters in each address that should be capital letters.

1. mr. william cross

   222 n. green st., apt. 2C

   urbana, il 61802

2. mrs. robyn apodaca

   814 morningstar circle

   brunswick, mo 65236

Write each set of addresses correctly on the envelope.

3. **From:** mrs. lynn jeffries
   401 peyton drive apt. 12
   salem, or 97303

   To: dr. josh harris
   707 n. beach st.
   seattle, wa 98110

   _____
   _____
   _____

              _____
              _____
              _____

4. **From:** The Mayfair Company
   525 Enterprise Way, 3rd Floor
   Mobile, AL 36611

   To: Mrs. Tonya Lyons
   1429 W. Arrowhead Ave.
   Taos, NM 87571

   _____
   _____
   _____

              _____
              _____
              _____

© Loyola Press. Voyages in English   Grade 3

For additional help, review pages 176–177 in your textbook or visit www.voyagesinenglish.com.

7.11 Direct Quotations

A **direct quotation** contains the exact words a person says. Use quotation marks before and after the words of a speaker. Use a comma to set off what is said from the rest of the sentence.

Add a comma to separate what is being said from the rest of the sentence.

1. Ms. Price said "Tell me about your display."

2. Trevor said "This is a diorama."

3. "This display shows a forest habitat" explained Deion.

4. Mr. White asked "Who knows an interesting animal fact?"

5. Mike replied "Kangaroos need very little water to survive."

6. "They get water from the plants they eat" added Michelle.

Add quotation marks to each sentence to show the person's exact words.

7. Bill said, These are photos of my rafting trip.

8. The book fair starts today, announced Mrs. Lane.

9. Serena asked, What is your favorite food?

10. Anthony responded, My favorite food is meat loaf.

11. That movie was awesome! exclaimed Tony.

12. These gloves keep my hands warm, explained Lorraine.

13. A. J. suggested, We could have a car wash to raise money.

Rewrite each sentence, adding commas and quotation marks.

14. Bethany said Frogs catch flying animals.

_____

15. They eat worms and snails too added Chad.

_____

16. They catch flies with their sticky tongues explained Lamar.

_____

© Loyola Press. Voyages in English   Grade 3

For additional help, review pages 178–179 in your textbook or visit www.voyagesinenglish.com.

SECTION 8 Daily Maintenance

8.1 **Valerie feeds the hungry rabbits.**

1. Which word is a verb?   _____

2. Is the verb an action verb or a being verb?   _____

3. What is the plural noun?   _____

4. Diagram the sentence here.

8.2 **Rob's backpack is blue.**

1. Is the subject simple or compound?   _____

2. Which word is a possessive noun?   _____

3. Which word is a subject complement?   _____

4. Diagram the sentence here.

8.3 **The students earned the best scores.**

1. What tense is the verb?   _____

2. Which part of speech is *The*?   _____

3. Is *best* an adverb or an adjective?   _____

4. Diagram the sentence here.

© Loyola Press. Voyages in English   Grade 3

8.4 **Yesterday we bought new clothes.**

1. Which word is a pronoun?   _____

2. What is the simple predicate?   _____

3. Which word is an adjective?   _____

4. Diagram the sentence here.

8.5 **They might play volleyball.**

1. Is the pronoun singular or plural?   _____

2. Which word is a helping verb?   _____

3. Is *volleyball* used as an adjective or a noun?   _____

4. Diagram the sentence here.

8.6 **Lisa and James are studying quietly.**

1. Is the subject simple or compound?   _____

2. What is the verb phrase?   _____

3. Which word is an adverb?   _____

4. Diagram the sentence here.

© Loyola Press. Voyages in English   Grade 3

8.7 **My parents will attend the recital.**

    1. Which word is a possessive adjective?   _____

    2. What tense is the verb phrase?   _____

    3. Is the plural noun regular or irregular?   _____

    4. Diagram the sentence here.

8.8 **Bruce often tells silly jokes.**

    1. Is *Bruce* a proper noun or a proper adjective?   _____

    2. Which word is a descriptive adjective?   _____

    3. Is *often* a helping verb or an adverb?   _____

    4. Diagram the sentence here.

8.9 **He is holding the biggest puppy.**

    1. Which word is a present participle?   _____

    2. Which word is an adjective that
       compares two or more nouns?   _____

    3. Which word is an article?   _____

    4. Diagram the sentence here.

© Loyola Press. Voyages in English   Grade 3

8.10 **The pink slippers are hers.**

1. Is the sentence a command or a statement? _____

2. What is the simple subject? _____

3. What is the possessive pronoun? _____

4. Diagram the sentence here.

8.11 **The band marches and performs.**

1. Is the subject or the predicate compound? _____

2. Which word is a collective noun? _____

3. Which word is a coordinating conjunction? _____

4. Diagram the sentence here.

© Loyola Press. Voyages in English   **Grade 3**

8.1 Subjects and Predicates

A sentence **diagram** is a drawing that shows how the parts of a sentence go together. The **simple subject** of a sentence is usually a noun. The **simple predicate** of a sentence is a verb.

Diagram each sentence.

1. Jason runs.

2. Seeds sprout.

3. She danced.

4. Balloons float.

© Loyola Press. Voyages in English   Grade 3

For additional help, review pages 184–185 in your textbook or visit www.voyagesinenglish.com.

8.2   Possessives

The **possessive form** of a noun shows who possesses or owns something. The possessive adjectives *my, your, his, her, its, our* and *their* also show ownership.

Diagram each sentence.

1. Felicia's dress sparkled.

2. My cat purrs.

3. Birds' eggs hatch.

4. His phone rang.

© Loyola Press. Voyages in English   Grade 3

For additional help, review pages 186–187 in your textbook or visit www.voyagesinenglish.com.

8.3 Adjectives

An **adjective** tells more about a noun. An adjective tells how something looks, tastes, sounds, or smells. Adjectives can also tell how many. The articles *a, an,* and *the* are adjectives; they point out nouns.

Diagram each sentence.

1. A bear hibernates.

2. Many ships sailed.

3. Sticky sap drips.

4. Nervous patients wait.

© Loyola Press. Voyages in English   Grade 3

For additional help, review pages 188–189 in your textbook or visit www.voyagesinenglish.com.

Section 8 • 123

8.4   Adverbs

An **adverb** tells more about a verb. An adverb tells when, where, or how about a verb.

Diagram each sentence.

1. Stars shine brightly.

2. Young children play happily.

3. The team scored quickly.

4. Guests arrived early.

© Loyola Press. Voyages in English   Grade 3

For additional help, review pages 190–191 in your textbook
or visit www.voyagesinenglish.com.

8.5   Adjectives as Subject Complements

A **subject complement** comes after a being verb. Some being verbs are *is, are, was,* and *were.* A subject complement tells more about the subject of the sentence.

Diagram each sentence.

1. Elephants are large.

2. Jeff's shirt is blue.

3. The movie was long.

4. My grandmother is wise.

For additional help, review pages 192–193 in your textbook or visit www.voyagesinenglish.com.

© Loyola Press. Voyages in English   Grade 3

Section 8 • 125

8.6   Compound Subjects

A sentence may have more than one subject. In a sentence diagram, each subject goes on a separate line with a dashed line for the conjunction that connects the subjects.

Diagram each sentence.

1. Dolphins and whales swim.

2. Trains and planes move quickly.

3. Bananas and lemons are yellow.

4. Steven and Derek studied.

© Loyola Press. Voyages in English   Grade 3

For additional help, review pages 194–195 in your textbook or visit www.voyagesinenglish.com.

8.7 Compound Predicates

A sentence may have more than one predicate. In a sentence diagram, each verb goes on a separate line. The verbs are connected by a dashed line for the conjunction.

Diagram each sentence.

1. Phil swims and splashes.

2. The fans clap and cheer.

3. Alicia tripped and fell.

4. Skaters glide and spin.

© Loyola Press. Voyages in English   Grade 3

For additional help, review pages 196–197 in your textbook or visit www.voyagesinenglish.com.

8.8 Compound Subject Complements

Some sentences have more than one adjective used as a subject complement. To diagram a compound subject complement, you will need a line for each adjective and a place to write the conjunction.

Diagram each sentence.

1. Sam's legs are long and skinny.

2. The apple is tart and tasty.

3. Grandpa's truck is old and rusty.

4. My dog is small but brave.

© Loyola Press. Voyages in English   Grade 3

For additional help, review pages 198–199 in your textbook or visit www.voyagesinenglish.com.

8.9   Compound Sentences

Compound sentences—sentences that are made up of two smaller sentences—can also be diagrammed. Put two sentence diagrams together with a conjunction written on the dashed line.

Diagram each sentence.

1. My father pitches, and Candace bats.

2. The package is small, but it is heavy.

3. The doorbell rang, and the dogs barked loudly.

4. The movie was scary, and Mark screamed.

© Loyola Press. Voyages in English   **Grade 3**

For additional help, review pages 200–201 in your textbook or visit www.voyagesinenglish.com.

8.10 Diagramming Practice

A sentence **diagram** is a drawing that shows how the parts of a sentence go together.

Write out the sentences.

1. _____

| Actors | rehearse |

2. _____

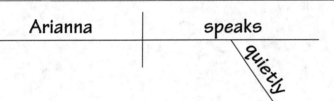

3. _____

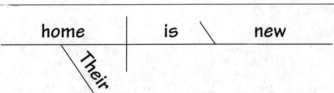

4. _____

bears | are \ brown

Some

© Loyola Press. Voyages in English   Grade 3

For additional help, review pages 202–203 in your textbook or visit www.voyagesinenglish.com.

8.11 More Diagramming Practice

A **diagram** is a drawing that shows how the parts of a sentence go together. Some sentences have compound parts.

Read each diagram and write out the sentence.

1. _____

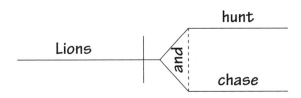

2. _____

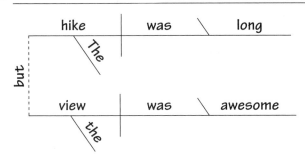

3. _____

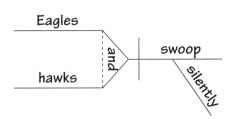

4. _____

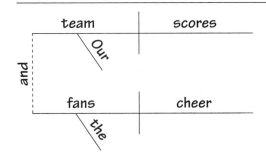

For additional help, review pages 204–205 in your textbook or visit www.voyagesinenglish.com.

Section 8 • 131

© Loyola Press. Voyages in English   Grade 3

What Makes a Good Personal Narrative?

A **personal narrative** tells about something that really happened to the writer. A good personal narrative includes interesting details that make the writing fun to read.

Circle the word or words that correctly complete each sentence.

1. A personal narrative is a (make-believe   true) story.

2. The topic of a personal narrative is the (writer   reader).

3. Personal narratives are always told from the (reader's   writer's) point of view.

4. A signal word used often in personal narratives is (*they*   *I*).

5. The events in a personal narrative are written (out of order   in time order).

6. An example of a time word used in a personal narrative is (*clock*   *then*).

7. A good topic for a personal narrative might be a (camping trip   recipe for soup).

Circle the topic in each pair that could be used for a personal narrative.

8. my waterskiing adventure   how to snowboard

9. making a birdhouse   our trip to the lake

10. the day I moved to a new city   the mountains of North America

11. the time I got lost at the mall   why plants need sunlight

Complete each sentence with a time word from the box.

before	after	during	first	until

12. I was scared _____ the entire roller-coaster ride.

13. _____, we hiked to the lake, and then we dove into the water.

14. _____ we washed the puppy, we dried it off.

15. I stayed with my friend _____ his parents arrived.

16. _____ I went mountain biking, I strapped on my helmet.

© Loyola Press. Voyages in English   Grade 3

For additional help, review pages 212–215 in your textbook or visit www.voyagesinenglish.com.

LESSON
2

Beginning, Middle, and Ending

A personal narrative is a story with a **beginning,** a **middle,** and an **ending.** Each part of the story helps the reader picture what happened.

Write *yes* if the statement is true and *no* if it is not true.

1. The beginning of a personal narrative tells what the story will be about. _____

2. A good beginning tells the reader what you have learned from the experience. _____

3. The middle tells how the story comes out. _____

4. The middle is usually the shortest part of the story. _____

5. A good middle includes many details and tells the events in the order they happened. _____

6. The ending tells the reader what the story means to you. _____

7. A good ending grabs the reader's attention and makes the reader want to read more. _____

Write *beginning, middle,* or *ending* to tell where each part would come from in a personal narrative.

8. Finally, I was home. I was glad the long day was over. _____

9. It all began on a bright, sunny morning. I had no idea what a bad day it would turn out to be. _____

10. The next morning I woke early. I was sure to catch more fish this time. I began to plan on my way to the lake. _____

Write sentences for an idea for each part of a personal narrative. Then write a title for your personal narrative.

11. Beginning: _____

   Middle: _____

   _____

   Ending: _____

   My title will be _____.

© Loyola Press. Voyages in English   Grade 3

For additional help, review pages 216–219 in your textbook or visit www.voyagesinenglish.com.

LESSON
3

Strong Verbs

A verb is often the action word in a sentence. A verb tells what the subject does. **Strong verbs** tell more clearly what the subject does. They create clear pictures in the reader's mind.

Write the letter of the strong verb in Column B that could replace each verb in Column A.

COLUMN A   COLUMN B

1. hold _____   a. glide

2. cry _____   b. sob

3. move _____   c. clutch

4. talk _____   d. smash

5. show _____   e. reveal

6. break _____   f. whisper

Circle the letter of the sentence in each pair that uses the stronger verb.

7. a. The eager shoppers <u>went</u> inside the store.

    b. The eager shoppers <u>rushed</u> inside the store.

8. a. The monkey <u>swung</u> through the trees.

    b. The monkey <u>moved</u> through the trees.

9. a. At night I <u>gaze</u> at the stars.

    b. At night I <u>look</u> at the stars.

10. a. The man <u>bends</u> to pick up his newspaper.

    b. The man <u>stoops</u> to pick up his newspaper.

11. a. Several boxes <u>tumbled</u> from the back of the truck.

    b. Several boxes <u>fell</u> from the back of the truck.

Write a stronger verb to replace each underlined verb.

12. The horses <u>ran</u> toward the finish line.   _____

13. My coach <u>talked</u> loudly to the umpire.   _____

14. The hungry children <u>ate</u> the snacks.   _____

© Loyola Press. Voyages in English   Grade 3

For additional help, review pages 220–223 in your textbook or visit www.voyagesinenglish.com.

LESSON
4

Colorful Adjectives

Adjectives are words that tell about nouns. **Colorful adjectives,** like strong verbs, paint clear pictures in the reader's mind.

Circle the letter of the sentence in each pair that has the more colorful adjective.

1. **a.** That was a good meal.

   b. That was a delicious meal.

2. **a.** I gently held the small kitten in my arms.

   b. I gently held the tiny kitten in my arms.

3. **a.** Your kitchen is spotless.

   b. Your kitchen is clean.

4. **a.** We were tired after the long hike.

   b. We were exhausted after the long hike.

5. **a.** I felt heartbroken when we lost the championship game.

   b. I felt sad when we lost the championship game.

Write a more colorful adjective to replace each underlined adjective.

6. Scientists study the old fossils.   _____

7. The new office building is large.   _____

8. We washed out the dirty trash cans.   _____

9. I walked quickly across the hot sand.   _____

10. Her sisters are very nice.   _____

Rewrite each sentence by adding colorful adjectives to describe the underlined nouns.

11. Snowflakes fell from the sky.

   _____

12. The students crowded around the robot.

   _____

© Loyola Press. Voyages in English   Grade 3

For additional help, review pages 224–227 in your textbook or visit www.voyagesinenglish.com.

LESSON
5 Dictionary

A **dictionary** is a book of words and their meanings. In a dictionary you can find how a word is spelled, the way a word is pronounced, and what a word means.

Use the dictionary entry to answer the questions.

> **plate** (plāt) **1.** A flat dish used for food [I put the toast on a plate.]
> **2.** Home base in baseball [The batter stepped up to the plate.]

1. What is the entry word? _____

2. Does the information inside the parentheses tell you how to pronounce or how to spell the word? _____

3. How many definitions does *plate* have? _____

4. Which meaning of *plate* is used in this sentence: I washed my dirty plate in the sink. _____

5. Which meaning of *plate* is used in this sentence: The umpire stands behind home plate. _____

Rewrite each list of words in alphabetical order.

6. feisty _____   **7.** timber _____

   wise _____   thief _____

   brief _____   tornado _____

   praise _____   theater _____

Write whether each word comes *before*, *after*, or *between* each pair of guide words.

WORD	GUIDE WORDS	
8. gown	**goodwill—grade**	_____
9. depart	**deport—deposit**	_____
10. miracle	**mild—mime**	_____
11. draw	**drama—dress**	_____

For additional help, review pages 228–231 in your textbook or visit www.voyagesinenglish.com.

© Loyola Press. Voyages in English   Grade 3

LESSON
1

What Makes a Good How-to Article?

A **how-to article** tells how to do something. It is important to choose an appropriate topic and give directions in a logical order so readers know exactly what to do.

Write *yes* if each statement is true or *no* if it is not true.

1. Before you write a how-to article, pick a topic.   _____

2. You should pick a topic that you know nothing about.   _____

3. You should explain the topic in a few short steps.   _____

4. Pick a topic that interests you but not anyone else.   _____

5. Giving directions to a place is a good how-to topic.   _____

6. Telling the history of America is a good how-to topic.   _____

7. How-to steps can be listed in any order.   _____

8. It is a good idea to number the steps in a how-to article.   _____

9. **Underline each topic that would be appropriate for a how-to article.**

    making French toast   folding an origami swan

    how bridges are built   how to get to the post office

    how to play dominoes   why a clean room is important

10. **Write *1–6* to place these steps for making a piñata in the correct order.**

    _____ Dip newspaper strips in the starch and use them to cover the inflated balloon. Leave a small opening at the top.

    _____ Pour the liquid starch into the bowl.

    _____ Blow up the balloon.

    _____ Get a balloon, strips of newspaper, liquid starch, a medium bowl, a pin, small toys, and prizes.

    _____ Fill the piñata with small toys and prizes.

    _____ Let the balloon dry overnight. Then use a pin to pop the balloon.

© Loyola Press. Voyages in English   Grade 3

For additional help, review pages 250–253 in your textbook or visit www.voyagesinenglish.com.

Chapter 2 • 137

Parts of a How-to Article

A how-to article has five parts: the **title**, the **introduction**, **What You Need**, the **steps**, and the **conclusion**.

Complete each sentence with a word from the word box.

list   order   title   introduction   tips   Materials   conclusion   steps

1. Tell what you will make or do in the_____.

2. The _____ tells what the article is about.

3. What You Need is a _____ of things the reader will need.

4. The _____ list what to do in order.

5. The conclusion might give _____ for other ways to do the activity.

6. The What You Need part is sometimes called _____.

7. Numbers show the _____ of the steps.

8. The _____ tells what readers made or did.

9. **Read the steps for making a leaf rubbing. Cross out the two steps that are not needed. Then write a list of the materials you need.**

Steps

1. Collect lots of leaves.

2. Do research to find out what kind of tree each leaf is from.

3. Lay several leaves on a flat surface.

4. Cover the leaves with a sheet of paper.

5. Count the number of leaves under the paper.

6. Rub a crayon back and forth over each leaf.

What You Need

_____

© Loyola Press. Voyages in English Grade 3

For additional help, review pages 254–257 in your textbook or visit www.voyagesinenglish.com.

LESSON
3

Dictionary Meanings

A **dictionary** is a book of words and their meanings. Some words have more than one meaning. A dictionary will give each different meaning listed with a number.

Circle the two meanings that are correct for each word. Use a dictionary if needed.

1. trunk
   a. an elephant's nose
   b. a large motor vehicle
   c. the rear compartment of a car

2. family
   a. something you know well
   b. a group of people who are related
   c. a group of related plants or animals

3. land
   a. earth or soil
   b. to come down from the air to earth
   c. a narrow road

4. grade
   a. a mark given for schoolwork
   b. a class year in school
   c. to finish a class

5. find
   a. to discover something
   b. money paid as a punishment
   c. a valuable discovery

6. character
   a. a person in a story
   b. a graph or table
   c. the sort of person you are

Look up each word in a dictionary. Write two meanings for each word. Then write a sentence that shows one meaning of the word.

7. **stage**

   meaning 1: _____

   meaning 2: _____

   sentence: _____

8. **jolt**

   meaning 1: _____

   meaning 2: _____

   sentence: _____

© Loyola Press. Voyages in English   Grade 3

For additional help, review pages 258–261 in your textbook or visit www.voyagesinenglish.com.

The Four Kinds of Sentences

The four kinds of sentences are **statements, questions, commands,**
and **exclamations.** Use sentences to tell something, ask a question, give
a direction, or express a strong feeling.

**Write whether each sentence is a *statement*, a *question*, a *command*, or an
exclamation. Write the correct punctuation mark at the end of each sentence.**

1. Does Kim know how to skateboard _____

2. Turn off the light when you leave the room _____

3. What an amazing sunset _____

4. How chilly it is this morning _____

5. Why are your shoes covered in mud _____

6. These tomatoes are from our garden _____

7. Athens is the capital of Greece _____

8. Bring me a glass of water _____

9. Bella's new puppy is a poodle _____

Use the directions to write an example of each kind of sentence.

10. Write a command you might hear from a teacher.

_____

11. Write a statement about a favorite place.

_____

12. Write a question you might ask a new student.

_____

13. Write an exclamation you might hear at a sporting event.

_____

14. Write a question you have about a famous person.

_____

© Loyola Press. Voyages in English   Grade 3

For additional help, review pages 262–265 in your textbook
or visit www.voyagesinenglish.com.

Name_____   Date_____

Compound Words

A **compound word** is one word that is made by putting two words
together. *Lighthouse, mailbox,* and *teammate* are examples of
compound words.

**Underline the compound word in each sentence. Then write the two words
that make up each compound word.**

1. Have you seen my toothbrush?   _____

2. This watermelon tastes sweet.   _____

3. Spike sleeps in a doghouse at night.   _____

4. Baseball is my brother's favorite sport.   _____

5. I brush my teeth at bedtime.   _____

6. The children are playing in the backyard.   _____

7. Did you hear the doorbell ring?   _____

8. The shortstop caught the ball.   _____

9. We draw on the sidewalk with chalk.   _____

**Make compound words by writing a word from Column B next to a word
in Column A.**

COLUMN A	COLUMN B
10. tooth_____	nail
11. rain_____	book
12. back_____	shield
13. hand_____	end
14. bed_____	bow
15. wind_____	paste
16. flash_____	print
17. note_____	light
18. toe_____	pack
19. week_____	time

© Loyola Press. Voyages in English   Grade 3

For additional help, review pages 266–269 in your textbook
or visit www.voyagesinenglish.com.

LESSON 1

What Makes a Good Description?

A good **description** uses strong, colorful words to tell about a person, an animal, a place, or an object. A description makes clear pictures in a reader's mind and tells how things look, sound, smell, feel, or taste.

Circle the letter of the answer that correctly completes each sentence.

1. A good description
   a. is always funny.
   b. forms clear pictures in a reader's mind.
   c. is both *a* and *b*.

2. A description tells about
   a. a person or an animal.
   b. a place or an object.
   c. both *a* and *b*.

3. Strong, colorful words
   a. make clear pictures for readers.
   b. put the sentences in time order.
   c. are not needed in a description.

4. Before writing a description,
   a. think about your audience.
   b. picture what you will describe.
   c. do both *a* and *b*.

5. To describe events in the order that they happened, use
   a. time order.
   b. space order.
   c. open order.

6. To describe something the way you see it, use
   a. time order.
   b. space order.
   c. closed order.

7. An example of space order is
   a. yesterday to today.
   b. first to last.
   c. top to bottom.

8. *Salty* appeals to the sense of
   a. taste.
   b. smell.
   c. touch.

9. A word that appeals to the sense of sound is
   a. *screeching*.
   b. *whispering*.
   c. both *a* and *b*.

10. *Prickly* appeals to the sense of
    a. sight.
    b. touch.
    c. smell.

© Loyola Press. Voyages in English Grade 3

For additional help, review pages 288–291 in your textbook or visit www.voyagesinenglish.com.

LESSON
2

Writing a Description

A good description is well organized and helps the reader picture what is being described. The writer uses words that help the reader easily follow the description.

Write *yes* if each statement is true or *no* if it is not true.

1. A good description helps readers feel like they are part of the story.
   _____

2. Something you can see, hear, or touch can be the topic of a description.
   _____

3. Something you can smell or taste would not make a good topic for a description.
   _____

4. The beginning of a description tells what you think or feel about the topic.
   _____

5. The middle of a description tells about the topic.
   _____

6. Never use time order in a description.
   _____

7. Space order is one way to describe a topic.
   _____

8. The ending might include a description of a new topic.
   _____

9. A good ending might explain why the thing being described is important.
   _____

10. The ending never retells what was said in the beginning and middle of the description.
    _____

Write why each topic would or would not be a good topic for a description.

11. The importance of freedom _____

_____

12. A favorite place _____

_____

13. Your costume for the play _____

_____

© Loyola Press. Voyages in English   Grade 3

For additional help, review pages 292–295 in your textbook or visit www.voyagesinenglish.com.

Chapter 3 • 143

Sensory Words

Sensory words appeal to the five senses: sight, hearing, smell, taste, and touch. Sensory words help the reader imagine what is being described.

Write each word from the word box under the correct heading on the chart.

round	pine-scented	sweet	loud
fuzzy	slippery	squeaky	flowery
sparkly	sour	salty	flat
bumpy	stinky	squawk	

1.

See	Hear	Smell	Touch	Taste

Write the sense to which each description appeals. Then underline the words in each sentence that are sensory clues.

2. The man's snoring is like the rumble of a freight train. _____

3. The frog is wet and slippery in my hand. _____

4. I arranged the pink, long-stemmed roses in a vase. _____

5. The scent of spices and apples lured us to the kitchen. _____

For each topic write sensory words that appeal to the sense in parentheses.

6. popcorn (taste) _____

7. hummingbird (sight) _____

8. fire engine (hearing) _____

9. kitten (touch) _____

10. fruit salad (smell) _____

© Loyola Press. Voyages in English   Grade 3

For additional help, review pages 296–299 in your textbook or visit www.voyagesinenglish.com.

Name_____   Date_____

LESSON
4

Five-Senses Chart

Use a **five-senses chart** to plan a description. Complete a five-senses chart with sensory words and phrases that will make your writing clearer and more interesting.

Write the words from the word box where they belong on the five-senses chart.

flickering light	rows of seats	whispering	soft seats
savory hot dogs	large screen	music	ringing cell phones
warm popcorn	musty floor	sticky floor	buttery popcorn
salty popcorn	icy drinks		

1.   TOPIC: AT THE MOVIES

Sight	
Hearing	
Smell	
Taste	
Touch	

Write *yes* if each statement is true or *no* if it is not true.

2. A five-senses chart helps you remember details about what you are describing.   _____

3. List all types of words in a five-senses chart.   _____

4. The format of a five-senses chart should always be a circle that is divided into sections.   _____

5. The headings of a five-senses chart are only sight, smell, taste, and touch.   _____

6. Include your topic as part of the chart.   _____

7. The chart should include one section for each of the five senses.   _____

For additional help, review pages 300–303 in your textbook
or visit www.voyagesinenglish.com.

© Loyola Press. Voyages in English   Grade 3

Synonyms

Synonyms are words that have the same or almost the same meaning. Use synonyms to add variety to your writing and to make it more interesting.

Write the letter of a synonym in Column B for each word in Column A.

COLUMN A		COLUMN B
1. calm	_____	a. secure
2. start	_____	b. request
3. discover	_____	c. begin
4. safe	_____	d. decrease
5. create	_____	e. peaceful
6. ask	_____	f. risky
7. shrink	_____	g. make
8. dangerous	_____	h. find
9. difficult	_____	i. hard

Use a synonym from the word box to replace each underlined word.

story	pile	broke	rough	naps	chair	clean	tasty

10. The tree's bark feels <u>coarse</u>.   _____

11. Jeff told us an incredible <u>tale</u>.   _____

12. Our cat <u>sleeps</u> on my bed.   _____

13. The ball <u>smashed</u> the window.   _____

14. Please <u>stack</u> these boxes in the garage.   _____

15. This dessert is <u>delicious</u>.   _____

16. Is this <u>seat</u> taken?   _____

17. Did you <u>wash</u> the dishes?   _____

© Loyola Press. Voyages in English   Grade 3

For additional help, review pages 304–307 in your textbook or visit www.voyagesinenglish.com.

What Makes a Good Personal Letter?

We write and send **personal letters** to people we know. Personal letters include five parts: the heading, the greeting, the body, the closing, and the signature.

Write the letter of the part of a personal letter from the word box that matches each description.

| **a.** heading | **b.** greeting | **c.** body | **d.** closing | **e.** signature |

1. This part gives the name of the receiver. _____

2. This part is at the bottom of a letter but above your name. _____

3. This part is the message of the letter. _____

4. This part gives the address of the writer. _____

5. This part can have several paragraphs. _____

6. This part is your written name. _____

7. This part is in the top right-hand corner. _____

8. This part often starts with *Dear*. _____

9. This part has a date. _____

10. This part may have the words *Yours truly*. _____

Rewrite each heading, greeting, and closing correctly.

11. your friend _____

12. 1721 west oak drive _____

13. dear aunt marie _____

14. Atlanta Ga _____

15. may 18 2011 _____

16. sincerely _____

17. 203 south grand avenue _____

© Loyola Press. Voyages in English   Grade 3

For additional help, review pages 326–329 in your textbook or visit www.voyagesinenglish.com.

Chapter 4 • 147

The Body of a Personal Letter

The **body of a personal letter** is where you write your message. We write personal letters to someone we know for different reasons. A personal letter will have a different order depending on your purpose.

Read each statement about the body of a personal letter. Write *yes* if the statement is true or *no* if it is not true.

1. The writer's address and the date are in the body of a personal letter.   _____

2. We write personal letters to people we do not know.   _____

3. Personal letters may tell about something that happened to the writer.   _____

4. People write personal letters to thank someone.   _____

5. If you need information from someone you know, write a personal letter.   _____

6. People write personal letters to complain about a product or service.   _____

7. All personal letters need to be organized.   _____

8. A personal letter should present events in the order they happened.   _____

9. It is a good idea to jump back and forth between different topics.   _____

10. You should never include questions in a personal letter.   _____

Write why each idea would or would not make a good topic for a personal letter.

11. to tell a friend about a river rafting trip

_____

12. to explain why you are returning a damaged product

_____

13. to thank a relative for a gift

_____

14. to request a coupon from a business in your community

_____

© Loyola Press. Voyages in English   Grade 3

For additional help, review pages 330–333 in your textbook or visit www.voyagesinenglish.com.

LESSON
3

Personal E-Mails

Some **personal e-mails** are like personal letters. People write e-mails to keep in touch with family and friends. E-mails provide a quick and easy way to share news and get information.

Circle the letter of the answer that completes each statement about e-mails.

1. People write e-mails to
   a. contact family and friends.
   b. share news.
   c. do both *a* and *b*.

2. There is no need to include
   a. the receiver's e-mail address.
   b. your street address.
   c. both *a* and *b*.

3. The subject line of an e-mail
   a. names the receiver.
   b. lists the receiver's address.
   c. states the message's topic.

4. Unlike a letter, an e-mail doesn't have
   a. a heading.
   b. a date.
   c. a greeting.

5. The body of an e-mail is arranged like
   a. the body of a report.
   b. the body of a personal letter.
   c. a how-to article.

6. An e-mail's closing might say
   a. *Your friend.*
   b. *Dear Mr. Benson.*
   c. both *a* and *b*.

7. Some e-mail programs include
   a. your signature.
   b. your photograph.
   c. secret messages.

8. Remember not to
   a. give out your password.
   b. open an e-mail from an unknown sender.
   c. do both *a* and *b*.

9. Some attachments may have a virus that
   a. could make you sick.
   b. could harm your computer.
   c. may improve your computer.

Write a possible subject line for each e-mail topic.

10. telling about winning a sports award   _____

11. thanking a family member for a gift   _____

12. arranging a weekend outing with a friend   _____

© Loyola Press. Voyages in English   Grade 3

For additional help, review pages 334–337 in your textbook or visit www.voyagesinenglish.com.

Compound Subjects

If two or more subjects in a sentence have the same predicate, they form a **compound subject.** The subjects of sentences with different predicates can be combined if the predicates are close in meaning.

Underline the subject in each sentence. Write whether the subject is *single* or *compound*.

1. My umbrella is in the closet.   _____

2. Jordan and Dante set up a lemonade stand.   _____

3. Cassie and her mom brought food to the party.   _____

4. The puppet show begins at noon.   _____

5. Regina, Ari, and I read comic books.   _____

6. We rode a tram at the zoo.   _____

Rewrite each pair of sentences as one sentence with a compound subject.

7. Christy plays the drums. Aaron plays the drums.

   _____

8. This ring belonged to my grandmother. This necklace belonged to my grandmother.

   _____

9. The dentist talked to the boy. Her assistant talked to the boy.

   _____

10. Corey looked for Patches. His sister searched for Patches.

    _____

11. A duck moved across the pond. A swan glided across the pond.

    _____

12. Buses went over the bridge. Cars drove over the bridge.

    _____

© Loyola Press. Voyages in English   Grade 3

For additional help, review pages 338–341 in your textbook or visit www.voyagesinenglish.com.

LESSON 5

Antonyms

Antonyms are words that have opposite meanings.

Match each word in Column A to its antonym in Column B.

COLUMN A	COLUMN B
1. young _____	**a.** easy
2. hard _____	**b.** far
3. right _____	**c.** end
4. dark _____	**d.** old
5. near _____	**e.** bright
6. beginning _____	**f.** wrong

Write *yes* or *no* to tell whether each pair of words are antonyms.

7. sharp dull	_____		11. neat messy	_____
8. begin start	_____		12. fast quick	_____
9. lose find	_____		13. remember forget	_____
10. pull push	_____		14. thin thick	_____

Write an antonym of the underlined word to complete each sentence. Use a word from the word box.

alert	cold	in	last	quiet	new	short

15. My brother is very <u>tall</u>, but I am _____.

16. The librarian asked the <u>noisy</u> children to be _____.

17. Trent is <u>first</u> in line, and Sue is _____.

18. I walked <u>out</u> the front door and went _____ the garage.

19. She replaced the <u>old</u> faucet with a shiny _____ one.

20. The <u>sleepy</u> boy was not _____ during class.

21. Gloves keep my hands <u>warm</u> on _____ days.

For additional help, review pages 342–345 in your textbook or visit www.voyagesinenglish.com.

Chapter 4 • 151

© Loyola Press. Voyages in English Grade 3

What Makes a Good Book Report?

> A **book report** shares details about a book you have read and how you felt about it. A book report includes facts and details that help readers decide if they would also like to read the book.

Write *yes* if a statement is true or *no* if it is not true.

1. A book report includes the complete title of the book and your teacher's name.

   _____

2. The author's name should be spelled correctly.

   _____

3. Explain why you chose to read the book in the beginning of the book report.

   _____

4. The beginning of the report should tell who the story is about.

   _____

5. Do not describe the setting of the story in a book report.

   _____

6. Tell what happens in the story in the beginning of the book report.

   _____

7. Tell just enough to make people want to read the book.

   _____

8. Do not forget to tell the reader how the book ends.

   _____

9. Tell what you think of the book in the ending.

   _____

10. Give reasons that support your opinion of the book.

    _____

11. Tell about parts of the book that you liked or did not like.

    _____

12. Include a list of other books by the author in the final paragraph of the book report.

    _____

Read this beginning from a book report. Suggest ways the writer could improve the paragraph.

> I read a book about an animal. Stuart lives with a family of real people in a city.

13. _____

    _____

© Loyola Press. Voyages in English   Grade 3

For additional help, review pages 364–367 in your textbook or visit www.voyagesinenglish.com.

LESSON
2

Character and Plot

Characters are the people, animals, and things in a story. The **plot** of the story tells what the characters do and what happens to them.

Use a word from the word box to complete each sentence.

idea	goal	important	villains	ending	thing
kids	animals	plot	not	long	

1. A character is a person, an animal, or a _____ in a story.

2. Story characters can be _____ just like you and your friends.

3. Characters can also be people from _____ ago.

4. _____ such as mice and horses can be characters in a story.

5. When you write a book report, tell about _____ things you learned about the characters.

6. The _____ of a story tells what happens in the book.

7. Most characters have a problem to solve or a _____ to reach.

8. _____ are characters in the story who work against others.

9. The _____ of a book tells how the characters solved their problem or whether they reached their goal.

10. A book report should give the reader an _____ of what happens in the beginning and middle of the story.

11. A book report should _____ tell the ending of the story.

Write whether each sentence describes a *character* or the *plot*.

12. Jessica is a shy girl who loves animals. _____

13. Brandon and Kyle search for clues in the backyard. _____

14. The knight fights and kills a fierce dragon. _____

15. Sherlock Holmes is a detective who solves mysteries. _____

16. Snowball, a playful white rabbit, always gets into trouble. _____

© Loyola Press. Voyages in English   Grade 3

For additional help, review pages 368–371 in your textbook or visit www.voyagesinenglish.com.

Chapter 5 • 153

LESSON
3

Parts of a Book

Most books have the same parts. Knowing what each **part of a book** contains makes it easy to find the information you need.

Circle the word or words that complete each statement about the parts of a book.

1. The (glossary   cover) includes the title of the book and the author's name.

2. The (spine   title page) connects the front and back covers of the book.

3. The (title page   contents page) lists the title of the book, the author's name, and sometimes the illustrator's name.

4. The title page may include the name of the (state   company) that published the book.

5. The (title page   contents page) tells the name of each chapter.

6. This page also tells on which page each chapter (starts   ends).

7. The glossary is a list of important (dates   words).

8. A book that tells a story (will   will not) include a glossary.

9. The index is a list of the important (topics   words) in the book.

10. The index includes (chapter   page) numbers to help readers find information.

Use the index to answer the questions.

INDEX	
core, 6	rivers, 15–16
deserts, 20–21	oceans, 15–17
forests, 22–23	sun, 4–5
mountains, 12–13, 26	volcanoes, 7–8

11. On which pages would you learn about Earth's oceans? _____

12. What topic is on pages 7–8? _____

13. Which pages tell about Earth's deserts? _____

14. On which page does the information about the sun start? _____

15. Which topic appears first—*rivers* or *core*? _____

© Loyola Press. Voyages in English   Grade 3

For additional help, review pages 372–375 in your textbook or visit www.voyagesinenglish.com.

LESSON
4

Compound Predicates

A sentence that has one subject and two predicates has a **compound predicate.** You can turn short, choppy sentences into smoother sentences by joining predicates with the word *and*.

Underline the predicate in each sentence. Circle *yes* if the predicate is compound or *no* if it is not.

1. Jana and Carl picked fresh vegetables.   yes   no

2. The boys collected their toys and put them away.   yes   no

3. The new Ferris wheel was scary but fun.   yes   no

4. We played games and watched a movie.   yes   no

5. I took family photos and framed them as gifts.   yes   no

6. Each player dribbled down the court and shot the ball.   yes   no

Underline the two verbs in the compound predicate in each sentence.

7. On the weekends I swim and ride my bike.

8. The outfielder jumped and caught the fly ball.

9. Our teacher stood in front of the class and read a story.

10. The leaves fell from the tree and blew across the lawn.

11. My brother plays the guitar and sings in a band.

12. The ball bounced over the fence and rolled down the hill.

Write a sentence that uses each pair of verbs as a compound predicate.

13. dig, plant _____

_____

14. sang, danced _____

_____

15. hike, climb _____

_____

© Loyola Press. Voyages in English   Grade 3

For additional help, review pages 376–379 in your textbook
or visit www.voyagesinenglish.com.

Chapter 5 • 155

LESSON
5

Prefixes

A **prefix** is a word part added to the beginning of a word. Prefixes change the meaning of a word.

Underline the prefix in each word. Then write the meaning of the word.

1. repaint _____

2. unusual _____

3. reread _____

4. reapply _____

5. unbelievable _____

Write the letter of the meaning in Column B that matches each word in Column A.

COLUMN A

6. unable _____

7. reappear _____

8. rewrite _____

9. unbeaten _____

10. rejoin _____

11. uncomfortable _____

COLUMN B

a. write again

b. not comfortable

c. appear again

d. not able

e. not beaten

f. join again

Complete each sentence with a word from the word box.

| retrace | unsafe | repay | rebuild | uncertain | unloaded |

12. We had to _____ the shed after the roof blew off.

13. Helen will _____ the money she borrowed.

14. The hikers were _____ about which trail to follow.

15. I will _____ my steps to find my missing keys.

16. Dad _____ the car after our trip.

17. The bridge looks _____, so they found another way to cross.

For additional help, review pages 380–383 in your textbook or visit www.voyagesinenglish.com.

© Loyola Press. Voyages in English   Grade 3

LESSON 1

What Makes Good Persuasive Writing?

Persuasive writing asks readers to believe something or to do something. A good persuasive article presents clear reasons that show why the audience should agree with the writer.

Circle *yes* if the statement is true or *no* if it is not true.

1. A letter of complaint is an example of persuasive writing.   yes   no

2. A persuasive article needs to have a topic.   yes   no

3. The topic is what you want the reader to believe or do.   yes   no

4. In a persuasive article, the reasons you state help the audience understand how they should do something.   yes   no

5. Include at least two reasons why people should agree with you.   yes   no

6. It is not necessary to know a lot about your topic.   yes   no

7. Use research to identify reasons that support your ideas.   yes   no

8. The Internet is a good source of information for a persuasive article.   yes   no

9. The audience for a persuasive article will always be your classmates.   yes   no

10. Include reasons that will interest your audience.   yes   no

Write the letter of the choice from the box that would be the best audience for each topic.

| **a.** parents | **b.** school board | **c.** principal | **d.** coach | **e.** teacher |

11. Our school's library should be open after school. _____

12. The team needs new uniforms and equipment. _____

13. I should be able to have a pet. _____

14. Our class should not have weekend homework. _____

15. All schools should offer after-school tutoring. _____

16. I would like an increase in my allowance. _____

17. Every player should be given a chance to play in each game. _____

© Loyola Press. Voyages in English   Grade 3

For additional help, review pages 402–405 in your textbook or visit www.voyagesinenglish.com.

LESSON
2

Beginning, Middle, and Ending

A persuasive article has a **beginning**, a **middle**, and an **ending.** Each part of the article has a special purpose.

Use a word from the word box to complete each sentence.

| change | retells | reasons | paragraph |
| topic | think | opinion | |

1. The beginning of a persuasive article has a _____ sentence.

2. Tell in the beginning what you want the reader to do or _____.

3. In the middle give _____ why the reader should agree with you.

4. Write about each reason in a separate _____.

5. The ending of a persuasive article _____ the topic.

6. Tell what the reader can do to _____ things if he or she agrees with you.

7. Use _____ words to show that you feel strongly about your topic.

Read the question. Write a topic sentence that gives your position for a persuasive article.

8. Should students be required to do community service?

_____

_____

Write two convincing reasons that support each topic sentence.

9. Kids should watch no more than two hours of TV a day.

_____

_____

10. Students should not have to wear school uniforms.

_____

_____

© Loyola Press. Voyages in English   Grade 3

For additional help, review pages 406–409 in your textbook or visit www.voyagesinenglish.com.

LESSON
3

Idea Webs

An **idea web** shows the ideas for a piece of writing. An idea web lists the topic of the writing, reasons that support the topic, and ideas that support each reason.

Rewrite each topic and reasons for a persuasive article as a group of words in the correct places on the idea web.

1. Topic: More people need to participate in recycling programs.
   Reason 1: Recycling means less trash goes to landfills.
   Reason 2: Recycling takes trash and turns it into new things.

2. Topic: Our school should have more recess time each day.
   Reason 1: A longer recess would give kids more time for physical activity.
   Reason 2: A longer recess would give kids time to eat a snack or visit with friends.

Rewrite the topic for a persuasive article as a group of words in the correct place on the idea web. Then write two reasons in the correct places.

3. Topic: Students should not be allowed to bring cell phones to school.

For additional help, review pages 410–413 in your textbook or visit www.voyagesinenglish.com.

© Loyola Press. Voyages in English   Grade 3

Chapter 6 • **159**

LESSON
4

Compound Sentences

A **compound sentence** is two sentences that are joined together by a conjunction such as *and, or,* or *but.* The two sentences that are joined to make a compound sentence have ideas that go together in some way.

Underline the conjunction used to make each compound sentence.

1. I ordered a salad, and Claire ordered a sandwich.

2. Brandy plays softball, but her sister plays tennis.

3. Tareq can clean his room, or he can take out the trash.

4. The boys might ride their bicycles, or they might visit a friend.

5. The leader gave directions, and the scouts pitched the tents.

6. Jane is always late, but Matt is often early.

Rewrite each pair of sentences as a compound sentence. Use the conjunction in parentheses.

7. John can take piano lessons. He can take guitar lessons. (or)

   _____

8. I like Mexican food. I don't like the spicy salsa. (but)

   _____

9. Doug wrote the story. Trina drew the pictures. (and)

   _____

10. Mom washed the car. Dad mowed the lawn. (and)

    _____

11. Apples can be sweet. Apples can be tart. (or)

    _____

12. Wayne enjoyed the movie. I did not. (but)

    _____

Write a compound sentence. Circle the conjunction.

13. _____

© Loyola Press. Voyages in English Grade 3

For additional help, review pages 414–417 in your textbook or visit www.voyagesinenglish.com.

Suffixes

A **suffix** is a word part that you can add to the end of a base word to change its meaning. Knowing suffixes can help you figure out what words mean.

Write the letter of the definition in Column B that matches each word in Column A.

COLUMN A		COLUMN B
1. helper	_____	**a.** without hope
2. hopeless	_____	**b.** without end
3. worthless	_____	**c.** one who helps
4. teacher	_____	**d.** one who teaches
5. writer	_____	**e.** one who writes
6. endless	_____	**f.** without worth

Add -er or -less to the word in parentheses to correctly complete each sentence.

7. A mountain _____ needs plenty of strong rope. (climb)

8. His _____ words hurt my feelings. (thought)

9. The _____ kitchen sparkles and shines. (spot)

10. We buy eggs fresh from the _____. (farm)

11. The waiter was _____ and spilled the water. (care)

12. Who is the _____ of this car? (own)

13. Helen's shocking news left us _____. (speech)

14. The _____ has a table and chairs for sale. (sell)

Write a word with the suffix -er or -less that fits each definition.

15. one who speaks	_____	19. one who trains	_____
16. without doubt	_____	20. without taste	_____
17. one who reads	_____	21. without sense	_____
18. one who swims	_____	22. without pain	_____

© Loyola Press. Voyages in English   Grade 3

LESSON
1

What Makes Good Realistic Fiction?

Realistic fiction tells about people and events that could be true, even though they are not.

Read each statement about realistic fiction. Write *yes* if the statement is true or *no* if it is not true.

1. Realistic fiction tells about people who could be real but are not. _____

2. Adventure stories and mysteries cannot be realistic fiction. _____

3. The characters in realistic fiction are always talking animals. _____

4. The setting is the time and place of the story. _____

5. Realistic fiction can take place in the past or in the present. _____

6. The setting of realistic fiction can be almost anywhere. _____

7. Characters in realistic fiction do not have problems. _____

8. A plot only has a beginning and an ending. _____

9. The plot begins when the character solves the problem. _____

10. Realistic fiction may tell what happens after the problem is solved. _____

Write whether or not each character or setting would be good for a realistic fiction story. Explain your answer.

11. a girl who finds a lost treasure

_____

12. a make-believe planet where people can fly

_____

13. a man who tells tall tales that aren't true

_____

14. a talking dog and its pet flea

_____

15. a tropical island

_____

© Loyola Press. Voyages in English   Grade 3

For additional help, review pages 440–443 in your textbook or visit www.voyagesinenglish.com.

LESSON 2

Characters

Realistic fiction tells about the main **characters.** You can help readers care about your characters by telling what the characters are like.

Use a word from the word box to complete each statement about characters.

| learn | say | appearance | feeling | differently | picture |

1. Readers can "see" characters when you tell about their _____.

2. Good descriptions help readers _____ the characters clearly.

3. Dialogue is what the characters _____ in a story.

4. Words that tell how a character is speaking, such as *shouted* and *groaned*, help readers know how this character is _____.

5. Readers _____ about characters from the things they do.

6. Characters might also act _____ when something happens.

Think about a character from a book you have read. Complete the chart with details that helped you picture and care about this character.

Appearance	Dialogue	Actions
_____	_____	_____
_____	_____	_____
_____	_____	_____
_____	_____	_____
_____	_____	_____
_____	_____	_____
_____	_____	_____
_____	_____	_____

© Loyola Press. Voyages in English   Grade 3

For additional help, review pages 444–447 in your textbook or visit www.voyagesinenglish.com.

LESSON 3 Dialogue

> **Dialogue** lets readers know the exact words a character says. Quotation marks show which words a character said. Dialogue tags tell who is speaking and how they said the words.

Add the missing quotation marks to each line of dialogue. Underline the letters to show where capital letters are needed.

1. wesley knocked over the paint, not me, said Sandra.

2. that's not fair! protested the girl.

3. He asked, how did you find me?

4. but I don't want to go to bed! whined the child.

5. Megan cried, my dog is missing.

Complete each sentence with a dialogue tag that fits what the speaker says.

6. Misty _____, "I won first prize in the spelling bee!"

7. "Look out for that branch!" _____ Dan.

8. The principal _____, "The third grade won the book contest."

9. "What is your favorite animal?" _____ Rachel.

10. The child _____, "I hurt my finger."

Complete each sentence with a line of dialogue that fits the speaker and dialogue tag. Use correct capitalization and punctuation.

11. The librarian whispered _____

12. _____ shouted the excited fans.

13. _____ groaned the rock climber.

14. The patient sobbed _____

15. _____ explained the teacher.

16. _____ cried the child.

17. The students pleaded _____

© Loyola Press. Voyages in English Grade 3

For additional help, review pages 448–451 in your textbook or visit www.voyagesinenglish.com.

Contractions

A **contraction** is a short way to write two words. The words are joined into one word with an apostrophe. The apostrophe replaces the letters that are left out.

Write the contraction for each pair of words.

1. I am _____
2. we are _____
3. you have _____
4. do not _____
5. I will _____

6. let us _____
7. we will _____
8. she is _____
9. they are _____
10. could not _____

Underline the words in each sentence that can be replaced by a contraction. Then write the contraction.

11. Alice has not found her harmonica. _____

12. They will meet us at the mall. _____

13. We have been there twice already. _____

14. He is my older brother. _____

15. It is time for dinner. _____

16. You should not walk home alone. _____

17. I have eaten Greek food many times. _____

18. Brad will not be late for practice again. _____

19. You are my best friend. _____

20. Was not that a great movie? _____

Write a sentence for each contraction.

21. let's _____

22. wouldn't _____

23. we're _____

24. you'll _____

© Loyola Press. Voyages in English   Grade 3

For additional help, review pages 452–455 in your textbook or visit www.voyagesinenglish.com.

Lines That Rhyme

Words that **rhyme** start with different sounds but end with the same sound. Many poems include rhyming words. A **rhyming couplet** is two lines of a poem that rhyme at the end.

Write four rhyming words for each word.

1. tree _____
2. pail _____
3. try _____
4. black _____

Write the letter of the word in Column B that rhymes with each word in Column A.

COLUMN A		COLUMN B
5. shout ____		**a.** peek
6. fish ____		**b.** bake
7. break ____		**c.** sink
8. sneak ____		**d.** restore
9. drink ____		**e.** pout
10. explore ____		**f.** wish

Write a rhyming word for the underlined word to complete each couplet.

11. If you count a lot of <u>sheep</u>,

    Do you think you'll go to _____?

12. If you met a cold, little <u>mouse</u>,

    Would you give it a blanket from inside your _____?

13. Wouldn't it be funny to see a <u>whale</u>

    Carry a bag of letters and deliver the _____?

14. If you gave a shovel to a <u>pig</u>,

    Do you think it would help you _____?

© Loyola Press. Voyages in English   Grade 3

For additional help, review pages 456–459 in your textbook or visit www.voyagesinenglish.com.

What Makes a Good Research Report?

A **research report** is a kind of writing that gives facts about one topic. A research report uses formal language and includes a well-organized introduction, body, and conclusion.

Read each statement about a research report. Write *yes* if the statement is true or *no* if it is not true.

1. A research report gives opinions about one topic. _____

2. A research report uses informal language. _____

3. The topic of a research report should be narrow enough to cover in one or two paragraphs. _____

4. The introduction of a research report grabs the readers' attention and tells about the topic. _____

5. The topic sentence states the topic. _____

6. Details about the topic are given in the introduction. _____

7. Information in a research report can come from different sources. _____

8. Details that are alike are grouped together in paragraphs. _____

9. The conclusion sums up the information in the report. _____

10. A good conclusion supports your opinion. _____

11. Books, magazines, and encyclopedias are all good sources of information for a research report. _____

12. Web sites are not reliable sources for a research report. _____

13. You should copy facts word for word from the source. _____

Explain whether each idea makes a good topic for a research report.

14. the White House _____

15. the history of the universe _____

16. a childhood memory _____

17. Amelia Earhart _____

© Loyola Press. Voyages in English   Grade 3

For additional help, review pages 478–481 in your textbook or visit www.voyagesinenglish.com.

Chapter 8 • 167

Facts and Notes

It is important to find **facts** for a research report and take **notes** as you research a topic.

Circle the letter of the answer that correctly completes each sentence.

1. Find information for a research report in

   a. your classroom.

   b. your school library.

   c. both *a* and *b*.

2. Nonfiction books are about people, things, and events that are

   a. old.

   b. real.

   c. funny.

3. Nonfiction books are usually about

   a. a single topic.

   b. one setting.

   c. one character.

4. A good source of facts about many topics is

   a. an index.

   b. an encyclopedia.

   c. an atlas.

5. Magazines usually have the most

   a. interesting information.

   b. current information.

   c. important information.

6. Not all information on the Internet is

   a. correct.

   b. reliable.

   c. both *a* and *b*.

7. Look for Web sites written by

   a. other students.

   b. experts.

   c. both *a* and *b*.

8. One way to organize note cards is to

   a. put them in piles.

   b. shuffle them.

   c. both *a* and *b*.

Rewrite the facts about volcanoes in your own words.

9. A volcano is a mountain where lava, ash, and gas erupt from Earth's surface. Below each volcano is a pool of melted rock. When the pressure builds up in the melted rock, it rises and flows out the volcano as lava. The word *volcano* comes from the name Vulcan, the god of fire in Roman mythology.

_____

_____

_____

© Loyola Press. Voyages in English   **Grade 3**

For additional help, review pages 482–485 in your textbook or visit www.voyagesinenglish.com.

LESSON 3

Library Skills

School and local libraries are good places to look for information for a research report. It is important to learn how library books and other resources are organized and how to find each type of book.

Complete each sentence with a word from the word box.

reference	nonfiction	call	description
separate	electronic	library	fiction

1. Libraries _____ fiction books from nonfiction books.

2. To find a _____ book, look for the last name of the author.

3. To find a _____ book, look up the subject of the book.

4. Dictionaries and encyclopedias are examples of _____ books.

5. A library catalog lists all the books in the _____ .

6. Many libraries have replaced card catalogs with _____ ones.

7. A book's _____ number is like an address because it tells where the book can be found.

8. Some electronic catalogs include a short _____ of each book.

Explain whether each book would be a good source of facts for a report on the topic of sea stars.

9. *Sammy the Sea Star* _____

_____

10. *Let's Learn About Sea Stars* _____

_____

11. *Ocean Creatures Up Close* _____

_____

_____

© Loyola Press. Voyages in English Grade 3

For additional help, review pages 486–489 in your textbook or visit www.voyagesinenglish.com.

Revising Sentences

When you **revise a sentence,** you change words and combine ideas to improve your writing. Exact words make your writing more interesting. You can combine some shorter sentences to vary sentence lengths.

Rewrite each sentence. Use an exact noun or verb in place of each underlined word. Add adjectives and adverbs to make the sentence more interesting.

1. The leaf <u>fell</u> to the ground.

   _____

2. We watched the <u>car</u> race down the road.

   _____

3. A bee <u>flew</u> beside my ear.

   _____

4. The <u>animal</u> looked out of the darkness.

   _____

Combine each pair of short sentences into a longer sentence.

5. Cameron borrowed my skateboard. Cameron borrowed my helmet.

   _____

6. Brenda is stargazing. Brian is stargazing.

   _____

7. Revise your research report. Proofread your research report.

   _____

8. We can play checkers. We can put together a puzzle.

   _____

9. Gail knits a sweater. Paul reads a book.

   _____

© Loyola Press. Voyages in English Grade 3

For additional help, review pages 490–493 in your textbook or visit www.voyagesinenglish.com.

LESSON
5

Homophones

Homophones are words that sound alike but are spelled differently and have different meanings. *Deer/dear, ate/eight,* and *son/sun* are examples of homophones.

Circle the word that correctly completes each sentence.

1. I will (right   write) a letter to my friend.

2. The (hare   hair) hopped quickly into the woods.

3. Cherise wants to (be   bee) a lawyer.

4. (Your   You're) going to be late if you don't hurry.

5. The (plain   plane) leaves the airport at noon.

6. That boy is my neighbor's (son   sun).

Circle a homophone in parentheses in place of the underlined word or words.

7. The flower has a sweet <u>smell</u>. (cent   scent)

8. It is wrong to <u>take</u> things from others. (steel   steal)

9. A <u>female deer</u> grazes in the meadow. (doe   dough)

10. The <u>soldier</u> defends the castle. (night   knight)

11. A bird sits on the <u>tree limb</u>. (bow   bough)

Complete each sentence with a homophone pair from the word box.

here/hear	ate/eight	threw/through
hour/our	pause/paws	you're/your

12. I _____ the ball _____ the hoop.

13. _____ flight leaves in one _____.

14. Stay _____ so you can _____ the timer.

15. _____ meeting _____ friend at noon.

16. I saw the cat _____ to lick its _____.

17. Peter _____ _____ small pancakes.

For additional help, review pages 494–497 in your textbook
or visit www.voyagesinenglish.com.

Chapter 8 • 171

© Loyola Press. Voyages in English   Grade 3